All recipes in this cookbook contain either vegan or vegetarian meat. When we mention a type of 'meat' (without the addition of 'animal') we are referring to our plant-based meat.

NEW MEAT

A PLANT-BASED ODE TO 100 CLASSIC MEAT DISHES

THE VEGETARIAN BUTCHER™

José van Mil and Fleur van Mil | Photography Remko Kraaijeveld

NIJGH & VAN DITMAR

They say meat is meat,
The Vegetarian Butcher says: Hold your horses.

They say nothing good comes without sacrifice,
The Vegetarian Butcher says:
We're not sacrificing a thing.

From meat to its culture, from animals to its earth.
From taste to texture.

Meat is far more meaningful than just its taste.
Meat is the centerpiece that unites friends,
families and foes.
Meat is the bare boned meaning of life.

They say we must surrender it all.
The Vegetarian Butcher says:
Sacrifice Nothing

CONTENTS

FOREWORD

Back in 2010, in a quaint little butcher shop in the Dutch city of The Hague, the public was first introduced to The Vegetarian Butcher's plant-based meat products. The shop brought together both vegans and carnivores, who you could say come from different worlds. The Vegetarian Butcher created a new world for meat lovers, where craftsmanship and plant-based ingredients resulted in a true tribute to meat.

That is also the aim of this book: to celebrate the diversity that plant-based meat can bring, and that there is more that unites us than sets us apart.

To satisfy meat eaters' tastebuds, The Vegetarian Butcher has always believed that meat successors need to match to the taste, texture and nutritional content of animal-based products. This has been the guiding principle of the company founded by Jaap Korteweg, ninth-generation farmer and meat lover, who decided to go vegetarian so he could offer people the opportunity to enjoy the experience of meat while sacrificing nothing. For more than a decade, The Vegetarian Butcher has taken on mighty meat icons like sausages, burgers and mince and transformed them into satisfying plant-based versions.

For this book, we spoke with eleven top chefs and front runners to hear their thoughts on a plant-based future. Our special thanks go out to Jonnie and Thérèse Boer, Paul Bom, Asimakis Chaniotis, James Goodyear, Josita Hartanto, Erik van Loo, Andrew Pern, Ricky Saward, Roepa Sonai, and John Warrington. Each of them contributed their best recipe based on one of our products: our vegan Chicken Chunks, vegan Crispy Chicken Burger, vegan Chicken Breast, vegan Raw Burger, or vegetarian Meatballs. Most of the recipes in *New Meat* were developed by José van Mil and Fleur van Mil. We also compiled tips and tricks from our master butchers, terrific hacks that will help you get even more out of our products and make the most wonderful feel-good dishes.

So here you have it: *New Meat*. The one hundred classic recipes are irresistible, and all are based on the new meat. This cookbook will provide every meat lover with the key to unlocking old-fashioned enjoyment, each time they go into the kitchen.

This book is an ode to everyone who is part of the Food Revolution – the food lovers, the revolutionary tastemakers, and the meat lovers determined to live, and let live.

The Vegetarian Butcher

HOW IT ALL BEGAN

Jaap Korteweg, who was born in 1962, became a ninth-generation farmer when he took over the family farm at a young age.

When swine flu swept across Europe in 1998, Jaap was asked to store the carcasses of tens of thousands of animals at his farm in the Netherlands, right next to his organic potatoes, onions, carrots, and green herbs. He balked at the idea. That moment served as a catalyst, and Jaap set off in a new direction. He took a long, hard look at the system and saw that the way we treated animals had to change – and seeing that he was part of that system, he started with himself. So Jaap – who was a real meat lover – decided to become a vegetarian. That turned out to be easier said than done, because he still longed for the flavour and versatility of meat. He made a deal with himself: he was only allowed to eat animal meat when he was away from home. What happened, though, was that he found himself having more meals at the homes of friends who *did* serve meat. Clearly, this was not a long-term solution. So how could he keep eating what he loved without sacrificing animals?

Jaap started looking for another way, one that would allow him to continue to eat his favourite meat dishes. He reached out to scientists and producers of plant-based proteins with the aim of developing vegetarian meat that was indistinguishable from animal meat. Made straight from beans and grains, with no animal involved. More efficient, and at least as tasty. Together with innovative chefs, he pondered how to capture the flavour and other qualities of beef, pork, and chicken, with plant-based ingredients.

And they succeeded! On World Animal Day in 2010, in the Dutch city of The Hague, Jaap opened an old-fashioned butcher shop where craftsmanship and enjoyment came first – old-style, but with the meat of today. Interest in The Vegetarian Butcher's meat grew rapidly within the culinary world. In 2012, *The New*

York Times announced The Vegetarian Butcher had created 'fake chicken that's finally worth eating'. Other major newspapers noted the rise in popularity of the new meat with headlines that asked 'whether our products spelled the end of animal meat'.

This fuelled Jaap in his mission, and he continued to surround himself with dedicated, open-minded meat lovers who were knowledgeable about the traditional animal meat processing industry. By collaborating with food technologists and culinary experts, The Vegetarian Butcher's product range grew into what it is today. Because flavour always came first, The Vegetarian Butcher managed to get a hoof on the ground in the culinary sector. Chef and butcher Paul Bom even placed third in the 'Golden Meatball' competition held by a major Dutch daily newspaper. His meatball was the only entry made without animal meat. The Vegetarian Butcher's vegetarian meat products continued to win prizes, and the products were receiving more and more recognition.
Germany and the United Kingdom were also introduced to the new meat. Although the goal of becoming the world's largest butcher with the greatest impact was getting ever closer, much still needed to change – there was a lot at steak. Strangely enough, while in Europe there are still all kinds of subsidies for meat, some of the products with 'chicken' in their names landed on the Dutch political agenda, and a ban on meaty names for vegetarian products loomed. But with no valid arguments, the ban was swept off the table. The movement has continued to expand, and the demand for plant-based products is growing outside of Europe too. Countries around the globe are interested in the products of The Vegetarian Butcher, which are currently available in more than 45,000 sales outlets in 55 countries worldwide.

This increase in demand has also led to a greater demand for recipes and special ways to prepare the products. Here at The Vegetarian Butcher we are more than happy to comply, because the kitchen is at the centre of everything we do. After all, that's where it all began for Jaap, the meat lover who went vegetarian.

MEATY MYTHS

They say... rumour has it. There are many stubborn myths surrounding plant-based meat. So what is nonsense and what is the hard-boiled truth? Here are some common fables along with our experts' responses.

THEY SAY
'Vegetarian meat is a highly processed product.'

The ingredients we use for our plant-based meats are pretty simple. When making our products, we use methods such as heating, grinding, cooling, and mixing. For flavour, aroma and colour, we use natural ingredients like onion and garlic as much as possible. Animal meat consists mostly of protein, water and fat. For many of our products, we use a technique called extrusion to mimic the structure of animal meat. We use pressure, high temperature and motion on bean flour, to provide a plant-based protein with a meaty texture. Besides plant-based protein, the other two main ingredients are fat (for juiciness!) and water. We also fortify some of our products with iron and vitamin B12 and binders like starch and methylcellulose. Cellulose provides structure to the cells of plants – it's what keeps flowers standing up straight. The cellulose we use has been treated, so it can no longer be termed natural, but it's an approved additive that is used throughout the food industry. The ingredients we use, as well as the process, are known and safe. They are based on treatments that provide optimal flavour and texture. Meanwhile, we will continue our work in finding more and more novel ways to structure our meat with raw ingredients.

THEY SAY
'Soy is an unhealthy ingredient.'

Proteins are essential for our health, which is why plant-based proteins are the basis of all our products. We mostly use protein isolated from soybeans because they are very nutritious. Soybeans are a good source of high-quality protein, fiber, vitamins, minerals and healthy, unsaturated fatty acids. So go ahead and have another helping! As we are meat lovers, we want our plant-based meat to be as close to animal meat as possible, in both taste and texture, and soy makes this happen. Besides that, is has a relatively low impact on the environment and high nutritional value.

THEY SAY
'Animal meat is essential to your health.'

A growing number of plant-powered athletes are advocating veganism, encouraged by perceived boosts to their health and performance. There are clear reasons for this: plant-based diets are often more in line with nutritional guidelines, because they are lower in calories and contain more fibre and healthier fats. In addition, plant-based diets have been found to lead to more varied food choices. So, vegans and vegetarians are lucky ducks! Because it's important to get all of the right nutrients when you go plant-based, we make sure that our plant-based meat provides plenty of protein and additional nutrients like vitamin B12 and iron.

THEY SAY
'Vegetarian meat is no more sustainable than animal meat.'

Releasing the animals from the food chain is not just good news for animals; it's also great news for our planet. Today, about 75 percent of soy is used for animal feed.* This soy is then indirectly consumed by people through meat and dairy intake. On average, European consumers eat 61 kg of soy per year.** Two thirds of this is in the form of animal meat such as chicken, pork and beef. Only 5 percent of the soy grown globally is consumed directly as whole beans used to make products like our plant-based meat, or products like tofu. Because we make our vegetarian meat straight from plants like soybeans, The Vegetarian Butcher significantly reduces the pressure on our ecosystems. It's no bull: that's how it will enable us to feed more people with the same amount of natural resources.

*Soy Scorecard – Assessing the use of responsible soy for animal feed. Published in 2020: WWF – World Wide Fund for Nature, Gland, Switzerland.
**The hidden world of soy. WWF Report, published in 2022: hiddensoy.panda.org

TIPS & TRICKS

We asked our master butchers for more ideas on how to use our vegan Chicken Chunks, vegan Raw Burger, vegetarian Meatballs, vegan Chicken Breast, and vegan Crispy Chicken Burger. Let the following tips, tricks, and super-hacks from our experts inspire you to use our trusty vegan and vegetarian meats in new ways.

Our vegan **Chicken Chunks** are our most versatile type of meat. For that true meaty experience, fry them till they're brown and crunchy on the outside. Heat a frying pan over medium heat and add a thin layer of oil. Fry the Chunks golden brown on one side, avoid stirring them too often. Turn them over and fry them a little longer until they're heated through. Meaty, juicy, and crunchy too. Perfect when you're feeling peckish!

Our Chicken Chunks love to land in a sauce or curry: first make your sauce, then add the Chunks and heat for another 2 to 3 minutes. Before you know it, you'll rule the roost.

For delicious barbecued Chicken Chunks, marinate them first, then simply thread them onto skewers and grill for 4 to 6 minutes.

Did you know our Chicken Chunks can also be used to make a filling for ravioli and samosas? Or use them to make Sticky Chick'n: dust them with a little flour and potato starch, fry them in oil until crisp, and coat them with a sweet and spicy marinade! For pulled chicken, cut the Chunks into very thin slices, then marinate them in your favourite herbs and spices or dry rub, and bake them in the oven with a little oil. Add a spoonful of barbecue sauce as a finishing touch, and your pulled chicken is ready to go.

The Chicken Chunks also work very well in sandwiches, wraps, and salads. Simply heat the Chunks slightly before using. For dishes with longer cooking times, such as stews, you should add them at the end. If you have a smoker oven, you can make your own smoked vegan Chicken Chunks in no time.

And it doesn't end there: our vegan **Chicken Breast** is a real all-rounder. Fry each Breast in a little oil over medium heat until golden brown on both sides – the flavour is amazing. Or cut the Breasts into strips and stir-fry them along with some vegetables and teriyaki sauce. Our Chicken Breasts are also great on the barbecue: marinate them in barbecue sauce, then grill them for 4 to 6 minutes on both sides until golden brown.

More in the mood for old-fashioned grilled chicken from the oven? Go for it! Turn your oven to the highest setting and get out the rotisserie attachment. Grilling for 5 minutes on each side will be plenty. Or turn the oven to 200 °C and add the browned Chicken Breast to a creamy sauce, tomato sauce, casserole, or stew. No one will miss the actual bird!

You can use our vegan **Crispy Chicken Burger** to make a mouth-watering burger, Caesar salad, vegan filling for sushi or wraps, crispy vegan chicken sandwich, or bao bun in two shakes of a tail feather. Fry the Burger in a little oil until golden brown on both sides (about 6 to 7 minutes), or heat a convection (fan-assisted) oven to 200 °C, place the Burger on a baking tray lined with baking parchment and bake for 7 minutes.

For extra crispiness, you can also deep-fry our Burger: heat oil suitable for deep-frying to 175 °C, and fry the Burger for 2½ minutes until golden brown. Would you rather use an air fryer? That works, too! Heat the air fryer to 200 °C and cook the Burger for 7 to 8 minutes until golden brown. The following applies to all methods: after pan-frying, baking, or deep-frying, place the Burger on a metal rack to allow it to cool slightly and also keep the crust super-crispy.

Cut the Chicken Burger into strips or chunks and add them to any dish where you'd like a bit of crunch. Don't drown the Chicken Burger in sauce, or the breaded coating will get soggy. For the same reason, don't cover the pan with a lid when frying the Burger.

Finally, our vegetarian **Meatballs** are best heated in a bit of oil in a frying pan over medium heat. They will be heated through after about 6 minutes. This also works well in the oven: 10 minutes at 180 °C and the Balls will be ready to roll.

Can you make a sauce with our Balls? Absolutely! Make your sauce like you always do, then add them at the end and allow them to simmer in the sauce for at least 3 minutes. That way they'll be nice and warm.

Our Meatballs are an ideal addition to any snack tray, and we've got lots more tips for our Balls. Ever thought of deep-frying them before adding them to a sauce? This keeps the Balls wonderfully tender. Would you like to simmer them in a sauce or bake them in the oven for an hour or so? No problem! Just make sure that the Meatballs aren't right on top in casseroles, and on pizzas it's best to top them with a bit of vegan cheese. Although you don't have to fry our Meatballs before using them, this does make them nice and crunchy on the outside.

And then there's the vegan **Raw Burger**, which you fry over medium heat until it's nice and brown. This works best if you use liquid vegan margarine in a pan with a non-stick coating. Frying them in oil will increase the likelihood of spattering.

What about an old-school barbecued Burger? Brush the Burger with oil before putting it on the grill. How you top your Burger is entirely up to you, so let your imagination run free.

You can also use our Burgers to make kofta, meatballs for soup, or a filling for cannelloni. Try sprinkling the Burger with your favourite spice mix to add a different flavour twist.

Bon appétit!

Good to know

1 tbsp = 15 ml
1 tsp = 5 ml

In the recipes, the weight of tins and jars is the total (net) weight, not the drained weight.

250 300 350 400 450

REMSCHEI

WEEK DAYS

4 servings (main dish) 35 minutes

VEGAN CHICKEN CHUNK PIZZAIOLA

150 g sun-dried black olives
2 garlic cloves
4 large shallots
3 large ripe beef tomatoes
1 bunch (about 15 g) fresh oregano, or 1 – 1 ½ tbsp dried oregano
olive oil
freshly ground black pepper and salt
100 ml dry white wine
3 tbsp pickled capers
50 g vegan margarine
2 packs (160 g each) vegan Chicken Chunks by The Vegetarian Butcher
5 sprigs of flat-leaf parsley

Using a sharp knife, remove the stones from the olives (they don't need to remain whole). Peel and finely chop the garlic. Peel the shallots and cut them into rings. Cut the tomatoes into small pieces. Finely chop the fresh oregano, if using.

Heat a generous splash of olive oil in a high-sided frying pan. Add the shallot and fry over medium heat for 3 to 4 minutes until translucent and slightly browned.

Add the garlic and fry for 1 minute. Stir in the tomatoes and cook for another 3 minutes. Add the olives and oregano, and season with pepper and salt. Increase the heat to high. Pour in the wine. When it stops bubbling, add a splash of water and allow to simmer uncovered over low heat for 15 minutes. Stir in the capers and the margarine. Continue stirring until the margarine has been incorporated into the sauce.

Meanwhile, sprinkle the Chicken Chunks with a little pepper. In a different frying pan, heat a splash of olive oil and stir-fry the Chicken Chunks for 3 minutes. Add them to the sauce, and heat together for a few more minutes. Remove the parsley leaves from the sprigs over the pan (and also add a little more oregano, if you like).

Tip: Good served with bread or gnocchi and romaine (cos) lettuce with balsamic dressing. You can also fry a finely chopped red (bell) pepper and/or red chilli pepper along with the shallots.

Although the name suggests otherwise, this is not a pizza. So what is it, then? Vegan Chicken Chunks in fresh tomato sauce with lots of fresh oregano, made according to a traditional Neapolitan recipe. *Buon appetito*!

4–5 servings (main dish) 2 hours

VEGAN LANCASHIRE HOTPOT

500 g carrots (of various colours), plus some of the greens from the carrot tops (optional)
2 large or 4 small onions
800 g waxy potatoes
100 g vegan margarine
4 vegan Raw Burgers by The Vegetarian Butcher
3 tbsp vegan Worcestershire sauce
freshly ground black pepper and salt
3 tbsp white flour
400 ml vegetable stock (made with 1 stock cube)
3 bay leaves

Also needed: a fairly shallow round, oval, or rectangular (enamelled) cast-iron baking dish that can also be used on the stovetop, or a high-sided pan that can also be used in the oven; a mandoline or other hand slicer, or food processor with slicing disc.

Preheat the oven to 200 °C.

Peel the carrots and cut them into thick slices. Peel and finely chop the onions. Peel the potatoes and put them in cold water.

In the baking dish or pan, heat half of the margarine over high heat. Stir-fry the onion and carrot for 4 minutes. Add the Raw Burgers, and break this into chunks with a spatula. Stir in the Worcestershire sauce, sprinkle with a little pepper and salt, and stir-fry for another 2 minutes.

Sprinkle the flour over the mixture and stir in. While stirring, pour in the stock and bring to a boil. Taste, and season with pepper, salt, and a little more Worcestershire sauce if desired. Add the bay leaves to the mixture.

Slice the potatoes very thinly and place them onto a clean, dry tea towel. Don't rinse them! Sprinkle the slices with pepper and salt.

Arrange the potato slices on top of the mince-carrot mixture so that they overlap. Distribute small chunks of the remaining margarine over the potato slices (or melt the margarine and drizzle it over the potatoes).

Put the Lancashire hotpot into the hot oven and bake for around 1½ hours until done. After 30 minutes, lower the oven temperature to 160 °C. Sprinkle on some of the carrot top greens if desired. Serve on warm plates.

A traditional dish from North West England in which the meat and carrots are covered with thin slices of potato. In former times, this dish would have taken a whole day to make, and women would have often brought the pan to the communal oven to bake. But with the new meat, you'll have your Lancashire hotpot on the table in a matter of hours. Moovalous!

2 servings (main dish) 20 minutes

SPICY NOODLE SOUP WITH VEGAN CHICKEN CHUNKS

1 garlic clove
a small piece (about 25 g) of fresh ginger
1 small red chilli pepper
4 spring onions
1 carrot
1 tomato
1 Shanghai bok choy or part of a regular bok choy
1 ½ tsp curry powder
1 pack (160 g) vegan Chicken Chunks by The Vegetarian Butcher
groundnut (peanut) or sunflower oil
2 tsp hot thick pepper sauce (such as sambal oelek)
750 ml vegetable stock
2–3 tbsp sweet soy sauce (such as Indonesian kecap manis, or thick Chinese sweet soy sauce)
150 g rice noodles
10 sprigs of fresh coriander (cilantro)
a few drops of sesame oil

Also needed: wok

Peel and finely chop the garlic. Peel and grate the ginger. Remove the stem and seeds of the red pepper and slice into thin rings. Cut the spring onions diagonally into thin rings; reserve some of the green rings for garnishing the soup. Peel the carrot and cut into very thin strips.

Chop the tomato. Leave the smaller green bok choy leaves whole; cut the larger ones into pieces and slice the white stems into thin arches.

Mix the curry powder into the Chicken Chunks. Place a wok over high heat and add a splash of oil. Add the Chicken Chunks to the wok along with the ginger, chilli pepper rings, most of the spring onion, and the carrot strips and stir-fry for 3 minutes. Add the chopped tomato, the white bok choy stem slices, and 1 teaspoon hot pepper sauce. Stir-fry for 1 minute more.

Pour in the stock and 2 tablespoons sweet soy sauce and bring to a boil. Add the green bok choy leaves and allow to cook gently for a few minutes.

Meanwhile, cook the noodles until done according to the packet instructions. Tip the noodles into a colander, rinse with cold water, and allow to drain.

Taste the soup and add a little more sweet soy sauce and hot pepper sauce if you like. Divide the noodles over 2 large bowls, and add the soup with Chicken Chunks. Tear the fresh coriander leaves into pieces over the bowls, sprinkle with the reserved spring onions, and drizzle with a little sesame oil.

You'll be all set with this hearty one-pot soup with vegan Chicken Chunks. This soup is ideal for using up those leftovers in the fridge. You can adapt it to any season, so let your inspiration run like a free-range chicken.

4 servings (main dish) 30 minutes

FLEMISH WATERZOOI WITH VEGAN CHICKEN CHUNKS

600 g firm, thin-skinned (new) potatoes
300 g carrots
6 celery stalks
2 small leeks
5 sprigs of fresh tarragon or 1 ½ tsp dried tarragon
50 g vegan margarine
2 packs (160 g each) vegan Chicken Chunks by The Vegetarian Butcher
300 ml hot vegetable stock
250 ml vegan cooking cream
freshly ground black pepper and salt
10 sprigs of flat-leaf parsley or chervil

Clean all of the vegetables. Cut the unpeeled potatoes into quarters. Cut the carrots into quarters lengthwise. Slice the celery into wide arches, and the leeks into wide rings. Coarsely chop the fresh tarragon leaves, if using.

Melt the margarine in a high-sided pan over low heat – don't let it brown! Add the Chicken Chunks and fry for 2 minutes. Remove from the pan and set aside. Without cleaning the pan, add the vegetables and the tarragon and fry for 5 minutes over low heat, but don't allow them to brown. Add the potatoes.

Pour in the hot vegetable stock and cooking cream. Bring nearly to a boil and allow the waterzooi to cook for 20 minutes. After 12 minutes, add the fried Chicken Chunks and allow to simmer for the remaining 8 minutes. Taste, and add pepper and salt as desired.

Meanwhile, coarsely chop the parsley or chervil. At the very end, stir this into the waterzooi, then ladle into bowls or deep plates.

Tip: If you'd like your waterzooi a little thicker, bind it with a bit of cornflour mixed with cold water.

Waterzooi is from the Flanders region of Belgium, and a true Flemish classic. This creamy, substantial soup was originally eaten by fishers, who made their 'zooi' (stock) from fish trimmings. But... all hens on deck! We are swimming against the current here and replaced the fish with our vegan Chicken Chunks.

WEEK DAYS

NOTHING

4 servings (main dish) 40 minutes

VEGAN BUBBLE AND SQUEAK WITH SAGE

4 sun-dried tomatoes in oil
1 large onion
2 garlic cloves
3 small sprigs of sage
50 g vegan margarine
4 Vegan Raw Burgers by The Vegetarian Butcher
1 ½ tsp curry powder
600 g leftover cooked pointed cabbage (sweetheart cabbage), white cabbage, and/or Brussels sprouts
800 g leftover cooked or mashed potatoes
freshly ground black pepper and salt

Also needed: non-stick frying pan (about 20 cm Ø); potato masher

Cut the sun-dried tomatoes into pieces. Peel and finely chop the onion and the garlic. Remove the leaves from the sprigs of sage and finely chop.

Heat the margarine in the frying pan over medium heat and stir-fry the onion and garlic for 3 minutes. Add the Raw Burgers along with the sage and curry powder. Break into chunks with a spatula and brown for about 4 minutes over medium heat. Add the leftover vegetables and stir-fry over high heat until slightly browned. Then transfer everything to a colander, drain well, and return to the pan.

Add the sun-dried tomatoes and the leftover cooked or mashed potatoes to the mince and vegetables and mash well. Taste, and season with pepper and salt. Stir-fry for 5 minutes more.

Then press down firmly on the mixture, and fry over medium heat until the bottom is lightly browned. Invert the bubble and squeak onto a plate. Then slide it off the plate back into the pan and fry until this side is also nice and brown.

Cut the bubble and squeak into wedges, and serve on warm plates.

Bubble and squeak is traditionally made from leftover cooked or mashed potatoes, cabbage and/or other vegetables, and meat, which are fried together. The name is said to refer to the sounds the mixture makes as it fries. Bubble and squeak is considered to be a real country meal. Super-simple, yet crispy and full of flavour!

4 servings (main dish) 35 minutes

VEGETARIAN MEATBALL AND ONION HACHEE WITH FRIES

1 kg oven fries
2 packs (170 g each) vegetarian Meatballs by The Vegetarian Butcher
500 g (about 4–6) onions
75 g vegan margarine
1 tin (70 g) tomato paste
2½–3 tbsp mixed spices, such as ras el hanout or Dutch hachee spices*
3 bay leaves
1 vegetable stock cube
2 tbsp red wine vinegar
2–3 tbsp cornflour
10 sprigs of flat-leaf parsley

*** To make Dutch hachee spices, mix together equal parts of black pepper, paprika (powder), and ground ginger, allspice, mace, and cardamom. Then add 4 whole cloves.**

Preheat the oven and bake the fries until crisp, according to the instructions on the package. Meanwhile, cut the Meatballs in half. Peel the onions and slice them into rings. Melt the margarine in a casserole (Dutch oven). When the margarine has browned and the foaming starts to subside, stir-fry the onions over low heat for 10 minutes until golden brown.

Stir the tomato paste into the onions and fry together for 1 minute. Stir in the hachee spices and add the bay leaves. Crumble the stock cube into the pan. Stir in the red wine vinegar and 300 millilitres of hot water. Add the Meatball halves. Bring nearly to a boil, and simmer over very low heat for 15 minutes. Mix 2 to 3 table-spoons cornflour with 2 to 3 tablespoons cold water to form a smooth paste, then add to the pan while stirring. Allow to simmer for another 2 to 3 minutes.

Divide the fries over 4 deep plates, and spoon the Meatball and onion hachee over the fries. Coarsely chop the parsley and sprinkle it over the hachee.

Tip: The flavour of the hachee will deepen even further if you stir in a tablespoon of dried mush-rooms along with the bay leaves. Or try replacing half of the water with dark beer or red wine.

Hachee is a classic Dutch meat stew, served with fries. But with our vege-tarian Meatballs, you no longer have to spend hours in the kitchen. You can have this on the table in half an hour, without having to sacrifice any culinary traditions!

‘I believe that our approach to our food has to change.’

Josita Hartanto has written three cookbooks and is chef at Lucky Leek in Berlin. The restaurant has been named Germany’s best vegan restaurant.

When I opened Lucky Leek in 2011, there were still very few vegan restaurants in Berlin – veganism was a long way from becoming the trend it is today. I soon realized that I could make my dishes more accessible, and help home cooks switch to a more plant-based menu. This inspired me to start writing my cookbooks. I’m quite proud of having introduced other people to plant-based cooking, and by doing so, raising their consciousness about the food we eat.

At Lucky Leek, we have a wonderful mix of guests. On the one hand, there are the vegans who want to share an exceptional dining experience with their friends. And on the other are the foodies who want to try something different and are curious about what that is, a traditional fine-dining restaurant that serves a five-course menu containing no animal products.

When I started out as a cook, I worked in a kitchen that prepared animal meat. But because I was learning more and more about how it was processed and the conditions in which animals were kept, at a certain point I decided I no longer wanted to be part of that kind of system. Seventeen years ago, I became a vegan. Ever since, I’ve done everything in my power to be as innovative and creative as I can, and to show that there is a real, and realistic, alternative to eating animal meat. Back then I also took it on as both a personal and professional challenge to work only with plant-based ingredients, and to develop a way of cooking that in many ways runs counter to the way restaurant kitchens usually develop their recipes and menus.
Just like The Vegetarian Butcher, I believe that our approach to our food has to change, and that producing food based on animal ingredients that come from factory farms will have disastrous consequences for us all.

It’s fantastic that The Vegetarian Butcher wants to make factory farming a thing of the past, and the only way to do this is to encourage people to switch to a plant-based diet.

My inspiration for the dish I’m contributing here comes from my desire to replace the meat in simple, everyday dishes with the new products now on the market. I dedicate my recipe to all of those who are actively working for a world without animal cruelty. Keep up the good fight!

JOSITA COOKS: **VEGAN CHICKERY STRIPS WITH GARLIC AUBERGINE**

2 servings (main dish) | 45 minutes

VEGAN CHICKERY STRIPS WITH GARLIC AUBERGINE

1 pack (160 g) vegan Chicken Chunks or 2 vegan Chicken Breasts by The Vegetarian Butcher*
5 tsp light soy sauce (Asian supermarket)
½ tsp hot thick pepper sauce (such as sambal oelek)
3–4 tsp cornflour
vegetable oil for (deep) frying
a piece (about 25 g) of fresh ginger
2–3 garlic cloves
2 lemongrass stalks
1 aubergine (eggplant, about 250 g)
1 red (bell) pepper (about 80 g)
½ courgette (zucchini, about 200 g)
2 tsp tomato ketchup
350 ml vegetable stock

Also needed: deep fryer or other pan for deep-frying; kitchen thermometer

* If you're using Chicken Breasts, cut them into strips. Place the Chicken Breast strips or the Chicken Chunks in a bowl, mix in 1 tsp soy sauce, the hot pepper sauce, and 2 tsp water, and marinate for 10 minutes. Then sprinkle in 2 to 3 tsp cornflour and mix well. Heat the oil to 180 °C, and deep-fry the strips or Chunks until they're golden brown and crunchy. Drain on kitchen paper.

Peel and mince the ginger and garlic. Finely slice the lemongrass. Slice the eggplant lengthwise into 2-cm strips. Cut the red pepper and courgette into bite-sized pieces.

Heat a generous splash of oil in a large frying pan over medium heat, and fry the eggplant strips until they have softened somewhat. Add the ginger, garlic, and lemongrass, and stir-fry for 2 minutes. Add the courgette and pepper, and fry for another 3 minutes. Stir in the remaining soy sauce and the ketchup. Add the vegetable stock, and bring to a simmer.

In a small bowl, mix 1 to 2 teaspoons cornflour with 4 teaspoons water and 2 teaspoons vegetable oil. Add this to the mixture in the pan and stir until the sauce thickens, 1 to 2 minutes. Add the deep-fried vegan chicken.

Serve with steamed jasmine rice.

Tip: To garnish the dish, cut courgette skin into long, thin ribbons. Tie the ribbons into a loose knot, and place on the dish. You can first soften the courgette ribbons in boiling salted water for a minute. Drain well.

4 servings (main dish) 45 minutes

PASTA CASSEROLE WITH VEGAN CHICKEN CHUNKS AND SPINACH

300 g pasta (gigli, fusilli, or penne)
25 g almonds
25 g shelled pistachios
2 garlic cloves
1 tsp fennel seed
1 tbsp olive oil
200 g pumpkin, diced
1 tsp dried oregano
2 packs (160 g each) vegan Chicken Chunks by The Vegetarian Butcher
200 g cherry tomatoes
freshly ground black pepper and salt
1 organic lemon
200 g baby spinach
200 g vegan cream cheese
100 g grated vegan mozzarella

Also needed: grater; baking dish (2½–3 l capacity)

Preheat the oven to 200 °C. Cook the pasta according to the packet instructions until just tender. Tip into a colander and drain well.

Meanwhile, coarsely chop the almonds and pistachios. Peel and finely chop the garlic. Crush the fennel seed with the flat side of a chef's knife or rolling pin. Heat the olive oil in a large frying pan, and fry the pumpkin along with the fennel seed, oregano, and garlic over medium heat for 5 minutes. Add the Chicken Chunks and cherry tomatoes and fry for another 5 minutes. Sprinkle with a little pepper and salt.

Remove the pan from the heat, and grate the zest of the lemon into the pan. Add the baby spinach, pasta, and cream cheese and stir well. Taste, and season with salt and pepper.

Spoon this pasta mixture into a large baking dish, and top with the almonds, pistachios, and grated mozzarella. Bake in the middle of the oven for 25 minutes. (If the pasta has cooled slightly, bake 10 minutes longer.)

Feeling peckish? This pasta dish with vegan Chicken Chunks, spinach, and pumpkin will give you something to crow about! Serve with a crisp green salad, and your menu is complete.

4 servings (main dish) 15 minutes

INDIAN GARAM MASALA CURRY WITH VEGAN CHICKEN CHUNKS

1 onion
2 garlic cloves
a piece (about 40 g) of fresh ginger
2 tbsp sunflower oil
1 tsp ground cumin
1 tsp garam masala (Indian spice powder blend)
1 tin (400 g) chopped tomatoes
100 ml coconut milk
freshly ground black pepper and salt
2 packs (160 g each) vegan Chicken Chunks by The Vegetarian Butcher
4–8 naan breads (or other flatbread)
10 g fresh mint
1 spring onion
1 cucumber

Peel and finely chop the onion and garlic. Peel and finely chop the ginger. Heat the sunflower oil in a pan over medium heat, add the onion and ginger, and fry for about 3 minutes until lightly browned.

Add the garlic and fry 1 minute more. Then add the ground cumin and garam masala and fry for 1 minute. Add the chopped tomatoes and coconut milk and bring everything to a boil. Season with pepper and salt.

In another pan, fry the Chicken Chunks on one side for 2 minutes over high heat, then add them to the curry. Allow everything to cook gently for 2 to 3 minutes.

Heat the naan breads in a hot oven (180 °C) for a few minutes, or in a dry frying pan over high heat, turning to heat both sides. Meanwhile, chop the mint leaves, and thinly slice the spring onion into rings and the cucumber into strips. Mix together. Serve the curry with the flatbread and the cucumber salad.

This Indian curry with creamy garam masala sauce is a spicy, chickeny classic. Fry the vegan Chicken Chunks for 2 minutes over high heat, then simmer them in the curry. No one will miss the actual bird!

4-5 servings (main dish) 2 hours

SCOTCH BROTH WITH VEGAN MEATBALLS

75 g pearl barley
125 g green split peas
50 g (split) red lentils
1 large onion
1 large leek
2 large carrots
2 medium parsnips
5 celery stalks
4 kale or green cabbage leaves
corn oil (or another neutral vegetable oil)
2 l vegetable stock (made with 4 stock cubes)
4 vegan Raw Burgers by The Vegetarian Butcher
freshly ground black pepper and salt

Put the barley, split peas, and lentils in a colander. Rinse them well with cold running water and allow them to drain.

Peel and finely chop the onion. Slice the leek into thin rings. Peel the carrots and cut them into cubes of around 2 cm. Cut the parsnips into 2-cm cubes as well (you don't need to peel them). Wash the celery stalks and slice them into wide arches; reserve a couple of leaves from the tops of the stalks. Wash the kale or green cabbage leaves and tear them into large pieces, removing any hard ribs.

Heat a splash of corn oil in a casserole (Dutch oven) or other deep pan and stir-fry the onion along with the leek, carrot, parsnip, and celery for 4 minutes over high heat. Add the stock, barley, split peas, and lentils. Bring to a boil, turn the heat down to low, and allow to simmer gently for 1 hour.

Shape the Raw Burgers into 12 balls. After the broth has simmered for 1 hour, add the balls along with the kale or cabbage leaves to the pan and allow to simmer for another 30 minutes.

Taste, and season with pepper and salt as desired. Serve in deep plates or bowls. If you like, you can sprinkle with the reserved celery leaves and/or parsley if you happen to have some.

Tip: You can also add 2 bay leaves when you add the stock.

A hearty broth to get you in a good mooo-d. You can make this substantial soup thinner or thicker by adding more or less stock. Delicious served with wholegrain, rye, or spelt bread.

4 servings (main dish) 60 minutes

VEGETARIAN MEATBALLS IN HUNGARIAN PAPRIKA SAUCE

2 large onions
4 garlic cloves
2 small red (bell) peppers
60 g vegan margarine
2 packs (170 g each) vegetarian Meatballs by The Vegetarian Butcher
5 tbsp sweet paprika (powder)
1 vegetable stock cube
2 tsp onion powder
freshly ground black pepper and salt
10 sprigs of flat-leaf parsley

Also needed: hand blender

Peel and finely chop the onions and garlic. Cut the red peppers into pieces.

Brown the margarine in a medium heavy-bottomed pan or casserole over fairly high heat. Fry the Meatballs for about 3 minutes until they are somewhat darker. Remove from the pan.

Lower the heat to medium. Add the onion to the cooking fat, and fry for 3 to 4 minutes until translucent. Turn down the heat to low. Add the garlic and pepper, turn the heat back up to high, and fry for 2 minutes more. Stir in the paprika and stir-fry 2 minutes longer over fairly high heat.

Meanwhile, bring 500 millilitres of water to a boil and pour into the pan. Crumble the stock cube into the pan and stir. Stir in the onion powder and a little pepper and salt. Bring back to a boil, then turn the heat back down to low and cook the sauce for about 30 minutes, until the pepper is very tender and a third of the liquid has evaporated. Puree with the hand blender until the sauce is relatively smooth.

Return the Meatballs to the pan and, still over low heat, allow them to simmer in the sauce with the lid partially covering the pan. Give them a good stir every now and then. Taste the sauce. If you like, you can let it reduce a little further, which will make its flavour even more intense. Season again with pepper and salt. If the sauce is very thick, you can add a little boiling water.

Tip: Serve with rice, orzo, or new potatoes. You can also use Chicken Chunks instead of Meatballs. Fry them on one side until crisp before adding them to the sauce.

Hungary has a long tradition of meat dishes. Perfect for this hack!
Jó étvágyat **('enjoy your meal' in Hungarian)!**

‘With strong convictions and the right people, you can go far.’

Jaap Korteweg – founder of The Vegetarian Butcher.

I'm a meat lover, and when I decided to stop eating animal meat at home and that I would only have a steak at friends' houses or in restaurants, we were suddenly eating out surprisingly often. People love meat – it's that simple. So I decided to look for a way that would allow them to keep enjoying their meat, but without making animals suffer. I didn't know anything about the food industry or the culinary world, and gave myself only a 10 percent chance of finding a wonderful alternative for animal meat. But if *I did* manage to do this, I gave the business a 100 percent chance of success.

One of my fondest memories is the moment when award-winning butcher Arno Wapenaar wanted to carry our plant-based meat in his shop. Another highlight was when our meatball competed alongside forty-two meatballs made from animal meat and was awarded third prize by a jury of butchers.

Because we want to reach meat eaters, we are strongly committed to the butcher's craft and artisanal ways of doing things. The aura that used to surround electric cars could never convince confirmed gearheads, but then along came Elon Musk and his Tesla, and this fast car won their hearts. You have to change people's mindsets, and you can't do that if you're serving them something that is unappealing.

Of all of our products, I find the vegan Chicken Chunks easiest to use, but lately I've also really been enjoying our snacks. I've had some construction work going on at our house, and I just love seeing these dyed-in-the-wool builders enjoying our vegetarian sausage rolls and other snacks.

The recipe I'm contributing to this book comes from my sister Nella and her colleague Elly, who run a catering service with products of The Vegetarian Butcher. All these years they've been there for me during presentations, making incredible plant-based meat dishes. It's easy to tell nice stories, but the proof is in the eating, and they made the stories come alive.

With strong convictions and the right people, you can go far. My own mindset is that I never assume something will be a success, because then you set the bar too high and it's easy to get discouraged because you're afraid to fail. Not trying something you really believe in, now that is failure. When you are trying something new, you can never fail.

JAAP COOKS: **PESTO-PASTA SALAD WITH VEGAN CHICKEN CHUNKS AND ASPARAGUS**

4 servings (main dish) 40 minutes

PESTO-PASTA SALAD WITH VEGAN CHICKEN CHUNKS AND ASPARAGUS

125 g (sweet) cherry tomatoes
1 red Romano pepper (sweet pointed pepper)
1 small red onion
8 dates
1 garlic clove
olive oil
freshly ground black pepper and salt
250 g (spelt) pasta
250 g white asparagus
250 g green beans
1 pack (160 g) vegan Chicken Chunks by The Vegetarian Butcher
100 g vegan green pesto

Cut the cherry tomatoes in half. Cut the Romano pepper in half lengthwise, remove the stem and the seeds and membrane, and cut into chunks. Peel the onion and slice into rings. Pit and slice the dates. Peel the garlic and squeeze through a garlic press into a large serving dish.

Mix the garlic with a splash of olive oil and the tomatoes, Romano pepper, and dates. Add pepper and salt, mix together, and allow to stand for 30 minutes.

Cook the pasta according to the packet instructions until done. Tip into a colander, drain, and allow to cool slightly.

Meanwhile, peel the asparagus, and break off the woody bottoms of the spears (a few cm). Cut the asparagus into pieces of about 7 cm. Cook them in a pan with a generous layer of salted water for 15 minutes until done. Add the green beans 5 minutes before the asparagus are ready, bring to a boil, and cook for another 5 minutes. Transfer the asparagus and green beans from the water to a colander, and allow to cool slightly. Heat a splash of olive oil in a frying pan and stir-fry the Chicken Chunks over medium heat for 5 to 6 minutes until crisp.

Add the asparagus and green beans to the pepper salad along with the pasta and pesto. Stir in the Chicken Chunks and top with the onion rings.

4 servings (main dish) 30 minutes

VEGAN CHICKEN KORMA WITH ALMONDS

1 onion
2 garlic cloves
a piece (about 50 g) fresh ginger
4 vegan Chicken Breasts by The Vegetarian Butcher
2 tbsp sunflower, groundnut (peanut), or corn oil
6 tbsp korma spice paste
50 g raisins
75 g ground raw almonds and 25 g whole toasted almonds
500 ml vegetable stock (made with 1 stock cube)
salt
100 g vegan yoghurt (at room temperature)
a handful of fresh coriander (cilantro) or flat-leaf parsley

Also needed: mortar and pestle, hand blender, or food processor

Peel the onion, garlic, and ginger. Cut them first into pieces, then grind or blend them together into a coarse paste. Cut each of the Chicken Breasts into about 10 long, wide strips.

In a high-sided frying pan, heat half a cup of water along with the onion-garlic-ginger paste and allow the mixture to simmer gently for 5 minutes. Add the oil and the korma spice paste, and heat for another 3 minutes over low heat.

Stir in the Chicken Breast strips, raisins, ground almonds, and stock. Cover the pan halfway with a lid, and allow the Chicken Korma to cook gently for 15 minutes more.

Meanwhile, coarsely chop the whole almonds.

Taste the Chicken Korma, and add more salt if needed. Stir in the yoghurt, and spoon the Chicken Korma onto a warm platter or warm plates. Sprinkle with the chopped almonds and the fresh coriander.

Serve with basmati rice or naan bread.

For chicken korma, the meat is not fried but cooked gently in the sauce. The korma spice paste and the almonds give this vegan chicken korma its rich, deep flavour. The breast of both worlds.

Vegan Chicken Chunk Piri-Piri

Vegetarian Meatballs in Sauce

4 servings (main dish) 25 minutes

VEGAN CHICKEN CHUNK PIRI-PIRI

2 garlic cloves
2–3 red chilli peppers
2 tsp smoked paprika (powder)
2 tsp fresh or dried oregano
freshly ground black pepper and salt
olive oil
2 packs (160 g each) vegan Chicken Chunks by The Vegetarian Butcher

Also needed: mortar and pestle or hand blender with blending cup

Peel the garlic. Cut the peppers in half lengthwise and remove the seeds and stems. Finely chop the fresh oregano, if using. Grind the garlic and chilli peppers in a mortar along with the paprika, oregano, ½ teaspoon salt, and ½ teaspoon black pepper into a thick paste, then stir in 5 tablespoons of olive oil. If you're using a hand blender, add the 5 tablespoons of olive oil along with the other ingredients and process into a thick paste. Put this marinade in a bowl, mix in the Chicken Chunks, and allow to stand for 5 minutes.

Heat a little olive oil in a large frying pan and stir-fry the Chicken Chunks for 3 to 5 minutes until lightly browned. You can also grill them on a hot griddle, in a grill pan, or on the barbecue for a few minutes, until browned on both sides.

Tip: Delicious served with a salad made from ripe tomatoes, onion, and parsley or fresh coriander (cilantro), and rice or wholegrain bread.

2 servings (main dish) 30 minutes

VEGETARIAN MEATBALLS IN SAUCE

2 shallots
1 garlic clove
olive oil
400 ml sieved tomatoes (passata)
1 vegetable stock cube
1 ½ tsp dried oregano
2 tsp agave syrup
1 pack (170 g) vegetarian Meatballs by The Vegetarian Butcher
8 sprigs of flat-leaf parsley

Peel and finely chop the shallots and garlic. Heat a splash of olive oil in a small heavy-bottomed pan or casserole over medium heat and fry the shallot and garlic for 3 minutes until translucent. Pour in the sieved tomatoes, and crumble the stock cube into the pan. Stir in the oregano and agave syrup. Bring to a boil, turn down the heat to low, and allow the sauce to cook gently for 10 minutes.

Then add the Meatballs and simmer them in the sauce until they are heated through, about 5 minutes. Stir in another splash of olive oil at the end. Meanwhile, coarsely chop the parsley. Sprinkle the Meatballs in tomato sauce with the parsley.

‘We are there at the source, and have a big influence on what gets eaten in the wider world.’

Ricky Saward is chef at vegan restaurant Seven Swans in Frankfurt, Germany. Seven Swans is the first vegan restaurant in the world to be awarded a Michelin star; it has also received a Michelin green star for sustainability. Many of the ingredients he uses come from the restaurant’s own farm, which is located nearby.

I try to win my guests over to vegan cuisine with the kinds of simple, familiar vegetables everyone has access to. The dishes I make with them allow these vegetables to shine. On the plate I go for simplicity, with the star players taking centre stage. Every award is an acknowledgement of all the blood, sweat, and tears, and for a chef, a Michelin star is the ultimate achievement. But from that point on, you have to continue to grow. It was fantastic to be the first restaurant to receive the Michelin Sustainability Award. The Seven Swans is a local, seasonal, sustainable vegan restaurant with a root-to-leaf and farm-to-table concept. We know our region and we know where what grows when. As a professional chef, your reach extends far beyond your own home kitchen – we are there at the source, and have a big influence on what gets eaten in the wider world. Now I’m chef at the first Michelin-starred vegan restaurant in the world, with our own farm that grows more than 350 kinds of vegetables and herbs – something I never would have expected when I was starting out.

My mission is to bring vegetables, nature, and a regional sense of place closer to our guests, and to make the world as a whole a better place. Permaculture is a part of this: I believe that we need to understand nature and interfere with it less so that harmony can arise – and that’s always a good thing.
Over the past few years I’ve heard pretty much all of the biases people have. Although I have never heard classics like *Vegetables don’t have any flavour, Vegetables are boring,* and *Vegetables are just for garnishes* from guests in the restaurant or at my table at home. So far, I’ve been able to convince every carnivore I’ve met of just how amazing vegetables are.

For me, the biggest challenge in plant-based cooking is eliminating animal fat. Cooking without milk, cream, and eggs, and with only regional products – that truly seemed like the Champion’s League. But I’ve learned that it’s really not that hard if you allow the vegetables to speak, keep their characteristics in mind, and understand how they respond to various techniques.
I dedicate my recipe to my mother. It’s so easy and quick to make. Just delicious. I’ve loved this since I was a kid. It’s good for using up leftovers, and this is my contemporary vegan interpretation of this dish.

RICKY COOKS: **THE VEGETARIAN BUTCHER FRICASSEE**

4 servings (main course) 45 minutes

THE VEGETARIAN BUTCHER FRICASSEE

200 g pearl barley
4 shallots
2 splashes of sunflower oil
2 chunks of about 25 g vegan margarine, plus 25 g extra
50 ml white wine
800 ml vegetable stock
freshly ground black pepper and salt
1 pack (160 g) vegan Chicken Chunks or 2 vegan Chicken Breasts by The Vegetarian Butcher
150 g carrots
150 g mushrooms
25 g flour
100 ml vegan cream
squeeze of lemon juice
1 sprig of rosemary
1 sprig of thyme
3 bay leaves

Wash the pearl barley several times until the water runs clear, then leave to soak for 20 minutes.

Meanwhile, peel the shallots and chop them into small pieces. In a deep pan, heat a splash of oil and a chunk of margarine over low heat. Add the shallots, and sweat them slowly until they are translucent. Then add the white wine to deglaze the pan, and allow the liquid to reduce briefly. Add the pearl barley and half of the vegetable stock. Taste, and add salt. Cook the pearl barley al dente according to the packet instructions, then spoon onto a baking sheet and spread out the grains so they will cool quickly. Loosen the pearl barley grains with a spatula occasionally to keep them from sticking together.

Place the Chicken Chunks or Chicken Breasts onto a cutting board, and cut them into bite-sized chunks. Heat a little oil and margarine in a frying pan over medium heat, add the chunks, and stir-fry for a couple minutes until golden brown.

Peel the carrots and cut them in half lengthwise, or into pieces of any size you like. Clean the mushrooms and cut them into bite-sized pieces.

Now make the roux. Melt the 25 grams of margarine in a saucepan over low heat, then add the flour. Stirring constantly with a whisk, blend the flour into the margarine and cook until it is golden and creamy. Very gradually whisk in the remaining vegetable stock (it doesn't matter if it's warm or cold). Heat to simmering, and continue to stir to keep lumps from forming.

Bring everything to a boil again. Add the vegan cream, mushrooms, carrot, rosemary, thyme, and bay leaves, and allow to simmer for 5 to 8 minutes. Make sure to stir occasionally!

Taste, and season the fricassee with a squeeze of lemon juice and pepper and salt. Add the fried Chicken Chunks and simmer for 5 minutes more.

Remove the bay leaves, rosemary and thyme sprigs before serving with the warm pearl barley.

4 servings (main dish) 25 minutes

CHOP SUEY WITH VEGAN CHICKEN CHUNKS

1 red onion
1 leek
1 small head broccoli
200 g (about 2–3) carrots
a piece (about 50 g) of fresh ginger
250 g white mushrooms and/or shiitake mushrooms
1 small red chilli pepper
1 garlic clove
1 tin (225 g) bamboo shoots (Asian supermarket)
sunflower oil
2 packs (160 g each) vegan Chicken Chunks by The Vegetarian Butcher
200 g baby corn (fresh or tinned)
400 ml vegetable stock
2–4 tbsp sweet soy sauce (such as Indonesian kecap manis, or thick Chinese sweet soy sauce)
3–4 tbsp cornflour
100 g bean sprouts
1 ½ tsp sesame oil
2 tbsp toasted sesame seeds

Also needed: wok

Peel the onion and cut into 10 wedges. Slice the leek into rings. Divide the broccoli into florets, and thinly slice the stems. Peel and thinly slice the carrots. Peel the ginger and slice into thin slivers. Clean the mushrooms and cut them in half. Remove the stem and seeds of the red pepper and slice into thin rings. Peel and finely chop the garlic. Drain the bamboo shoots.

Heat a splash of oil in a wok over high heat. Stir-fry the onion, leek, broccoli, carrot, and ginger for 4 minutes. Then add the Chicken Chunks, mushrooms, chilli pepper rings, garlic, bamboo shoots, and baby corn and stir-fry for 2 minutes more.

Add the stock and 2 tablespoons sweet soy sauce, bring to a boil, and allow to cook gently for a few minutes. Mix 2 tablespoons cornflour with 2 tablespoons cold water to form a smooth paste, then add to the pan while stirring until the sauce has thickened slightly. If necessary, add a bit more cornflour paste (made with the remaining 1–2 tablespoons cornflour and 1–2 tablespoons cold water). Stir in the bean sprouts. Taste, and add a little more sweet soy sauce if desired. At the very end, stir in the sesame oil and sprinkle with the sesame seeds.

Tip: Red chilli pepper is not just hot, it adds flavour. Are chilli peppers too hot for you? Try soaking the chillies in vinegar for 30 minutes. This will remove some of the heat while retaining the flavour.

Chop suey literally means 'mixed vegetables'. This makes it ideal for using up leftovers, and our vegan Chicken Chunks provide the finishing touch. You can vary the vegetables in this dish to make it just the way you like. Wing it!

4 servings (lunch or main dish) 25 minutes

VEGAN CRISPY CHICKEN BURGERS WITH QUICK APPLE-CRANBERRY CHUTNEY

1 small red onion
2 crisp sweet-tart Elstar or other apples
olive oil
1 small orange
1 ½ tbsp granulated sugar
4 tbsp (semi-)dried cranberries
2 cloves
freshly ground black pepper and salt
pinch of cinnamon
4 vegan Crispy Chicken Burgers by The Vegetarian Butcher

Peel the onion and slice it into thin rings. Peel and quarter the apples, remove the cores, and cut the pieces into chunks.

Heat a splash of olive oil in a frying pan over fairly high heat, and stir-fry the onion with the apple for 5 minutes.

Meanwhile, wash the orange and grate the zest into the pan. Cut the orange in half. When the onion and apple are cooked, squeeze the orange halves over the pan. Add the sugar, cranberries, cloves, plenty of pepper, a pinch of salt, and 200 millilitres of hot water. Allow the liquid in the pan to evaporate rapidly over high heat. Stir constantly! Add the cinnamon. Allow the chutney to cool slightly while you fry the Burgers. Remove the cloves.

Heat a splash of olive oil in a frying pan over medium heat and fry the Crispy Chicken Burgers on both sides for a few minutes until they're nice and crisp.

Arrange the Burgers on a warm platter and top with some of the chutney.

Delicious served with a mixed green salad.

For this recipe, the chutney is still a little warm – but it's also delicious cold served along with the Crispy Chicken Burgers. These Burgers will be flying off the plates!

2 servings (main dish) 45 minutes

ROTI WITH VEGAN CHICKEN CHUNKS

1 shallot
1 garlic clove
a piece (20–30 g) of fresh ginger
1 red chilli pepper
1 tbsp sunflower oil
1 pack (160 g) vegan Chicken Chunks by The Vegetarian Butcher
1 tsp ground turmeric
1 tsp ground coriander
1 tsp ground cumin
1 tsp garam masala (Indian spice powder blend)
chilli powder to taste
1 tin (400 g) chopped tomatoes
150 ml thick coconut cream (unsweetened; Asian supermarket)
salt
2 roti flatbreads or wholewheat parathas (Asian supermarket)
10 sprigs of fresh coriander (cilantro)

Also needed: wok

Peel and finely chop the shallot and garlic. Peel and finely chop the ginger. Cut the red chilli pepper in half lengthwise and remove the seeds and membrane. Finely chop the chilli pepper.

Heat the sunflower oil in a wok and fry the shallot, garlic, chilli pepper, and ginger over low heat for 5 minutes until they start to brown. Increase the heat slightly. Then add the Chicken Chunks and fry for about 4 minutes until golden brown.

Now add the ground turmeric, coriander, cumin, garam masala, and a pinch of chilli powder to the pan and fry for a couple of minutes. Next, add the chopped tomatoes (along with the liquid) and coconut cream. Let everything cook gently over medium heat for 30 minutes. The liquid should have reduced considerably so that the sauce is fairly thick. Season with salt.

Just before serving, heat the roti flatbreads or parathas in a dry frying pan over high heat for 2 to 3 minutes on each side. Put the rotis or parathas on 2 plates, spoon on the curry, and garnish with the sprigs of fresh coriander.

Tip: Delicious served with sweet cucumber pickles.

This vegan roti is based on a fantastic family recipe from the Indian/Pakistani kitchen. Birds of a feather flock together, so if you are with many and all into great food, we recommend making this dish for big(ger) gatherings.

4–5 servings (main dish) 45 minutes

NEW ORLEANS VEGAN CHICKEN JAMBALAYA

4 vegan Chicken Breasts by The Vegetarian Butcher
8 large overripe beef tomatoes
2 onions
2 garlic cloves
300 g flat green beans (runner beans)
2 green (bell) peppers
6 celery stalks, plus a few leaves from the tops of the stalks
corn oil
1 – 1 ½ tbsp Cajun seasoning
3 bay leaves
250 g long-grain rice
1 – 1 ½ l strong vegetable stock (made with 2 stock cubes)

Also needed: casserole (Dutch oven)

Cut each Chicken Breast into 6 large pieces. Cut the tomatoes into large chunks, and save any juice that is released in a bowl. Peel and finely chop the onions and garlic. Cut the flat green beans lengthwise into strips, the peppers into chunks, and the celery into arches. Reserve a few of the green leaves from the tops of the celery stalks to sprinkle over the jambalaya at the end.

Heat a generous splash of corn oil in the casserole over medium heat, and fry the Chicken Breast chunks until lightly browned. Add the onion, garlic, pepper, and celery arches, and stir-fry for 6 minutes. Add the tomato, and stir-fry for another 5 minutes. Stir in 1 tablespoon Cajun seasoning, the bay leaves, and the rice.

Add the juice from the tomatoes and half of the stock to the pan. Give it a quick stir, and bring just to a boil. Add the green bean strips, and after 3 minutes turn the heat to low. Cover the pan with a lid, and allow the jambalaya to cook for around 20 minutes until done. Check regularly to see if you need to add more stock – if the rice is dry before it is cooked through, add small amounts of stock as needed (if you've used all of the stock, you can also add small amounts of water).

Taste, and add more Cajun seasoning if desired. Serve in warm bowls or deep plates, sprinkled with a few of the reserved celery leaves.

Tip: Put a bottle of hot red pepper sauce (such as Tabasco) on the table so that everyone can add this to taste.

In New Orleans, jambalaya is traditionally made with tomatoes and is known as red jambalaya. The origins of jambalaya date back to paella, a Spanish dish brought to the United States by immigrants. For our version, we've gone for New Orleans-style jambalaya, made of course with luscious vegan Chicken Breast. Whether you are near or far, you'll find the new meat where you are.

2 servings (main dish) 20 minutes

VEGAN CHICKEN CHUNKS AND GREEN ASPARAGUS STIR-FRY

2 red onions
1 garlic clove
a piece (about 25 g) of fresh ginger
150 g sugar snap peas
150 g green asparagus
125 g Chinese-style egg noodles (mee)
1 tbsp groundnut (peanut) oil
1 pack (160 g) vegan Chicken Chunks by The Vegetarian Butcher
2–3 tbsp chilli sauce
3 tbsp light soy sauce
freshly ground black pepper and salt

Also needed: wok

Peel the onions and slice them into thin half-moons. Peel and finely chop the garlic and ginger. Remove the tips from the sugar snaps (and also pull off the tough string that runs along the side of the pod at the same time). Break off the bottoms of the asparagus spears if they are woody. Cut the spears in half lengthwise, then cut these halves in two.

Cook the egg noodles according to the packet instructions. Tip them into a colander and drain well.

Heat the groundnut oil in a wok over high heat, and stir-fry the onion, garlic, ginger, sugar snaps, asparagus, and Chicken Chunks for 5 to 6 minutes until the Chunks start to brown. Stir in 2 tablespoons chilli sauce, the soy sauce, and 1 tablespoon water. Taste. If desired, add another tablespoon of chilli sauce. Season with pepper and salt. Serve with the noodles.

Farm-fresh asparagus, sugar snaps, and tender vegan Chicken Chunks all go into this wonderful stir-fry for two. Fire up the wok and enjoy!

4 servings (main dish) 45 minutes

VEGAN CHICKEN AND CHIPS WITH HOME MADE RED SKIN POTATO FRIES

1 kg red potatoes, unpeeled
vegetable oil for deep-frying
(coarse) salt
4 sprigs of flat-leaf parsley
8 vegan Crispy Chicken Burgers by The Vegetarian Butcher
pinch of smoked paprika (powder)
splash of crema di balsamico (balsamic vinegar condiment)

Also needed: 4 pieces of newspaper; deep fryer or other pan for deep-frying; kitchen thermometer

Slice each potato into 6 to 8 long fries. Place them on a clean tea towel and pat them dry.

Fill a deep fryer with oil to the maximum level indicated on the fryer, and heat the oil to 150 °C. Fry the potatoes in 4 batches for 7 to 10 minutes, but don't let them get brown. When they float to the surface, they're ready. Allow the fries to drain in a colander lined with kitchen paper while you fry the rest for the first time.

Just before you're ready to eat, fry them one more time. Heat the oil in the deep fryer to 180 °C and fry in 4 batches until golden brown. Allow them to drain in a colander lined with more kitchen paper. Sprinkle with a little salt and give them a good shake.

Meanwhile, coarsely chop the parsley.

When the fries are ready, deep-fry the Burgers in small batches until crisp. Cut them in half. Divide the fries over the 4 pieces of newspaper, top with the Crispy Chicken Burger halves, drizzle with a little crema di balsamico, and sprinkle with smoked paprika and parsley.

Traditionally served on squares of newspaper, you eat our vegan Crispy Chicken Burgers and home made fries with crema di balsamico with your hands. These Burgers make headlines! For extra tartness, you can also use regular balsamic vinegar.

4 servings (main dish) 20 minutes

SPICY PASTA WITH VEGAN CHICKEN CHUNKS AND PESTO

1 garlic clove
1 large shallot
100 g pine nuts
3 tbsp capers, drained
50 g basil
about 100 ml olive oil, plus extra
freshly ground black pepper and salt
300 g pappardelle or tagliatelle
a small piece of red chilli pepper*
2 packs (160 g each) vegan Chicken Chunks by The Vegetarian Butcher

Also needed: hand blender with blending cup

* There are all sorts of chilli peppers, from mild to red-hot. See for yourself what you like and how much you want to add.

Peel the garlic and the shallot, and cut each of them into four. Put the garlic and shallot into the blending cup of the hand blender and process until fairly coarse. Add the pine nuts, capers, and basil and pulse briefly. Then add around 100 millilitres of olive oil a little bit at a time, blending after each addition. Taste, and season with pepper and salt as desired.

Cook the pasta until done according to the packet instructions.

Meanwhile, coarsely chop the red chilli pepper. Heat a splash of olive oil in a large frying pan over medium heat and stir-fry the Chicken Chunks with the red chilli pepper for 3 minutes.

Tip the pasta into a colander and allow to drain. Now transfer the pasta to a large preheated serving dish and mix with the Chicken Chunks and the pesto. Chowtime!

Tip: You can replace the basil with one or more other green herbs such as oregano, parsley, sage, or tarragon.

Just the ticket when you're hankering for a good plate of pasta. This spicy pasta with pesto is done in a jiffy, and you even make the pesto from scratch.

The Star
Inn

‘Vegan cooking has provided me with a whole new range of possibilities.’

Andrew Pern is chef and owner of three restaurants, including The Star in North Yorkshire, which has been awarded a Michelin star.

I had just heard that our restaurant had been named the third-best gastropub in the United Kingdom when The Star burned almost completely to the ground. Last year we celebrated our twenty-fifth year in business, so you could say that things did not quite go according to plan. But I don’t get upset easily – that wouldn’t be very helpful, what with three restaurants and seven children. Two of my daughters became vegan when they were still quite young, and for me – with my classical French training – that was a bit of a switch. How do I get all of that depth of flavour into my food without any animal ingredients?

I come from a farming background, so I’m used to working with the seasons. Many of my ingredients come from the foragers, growers, and hunters in the area. Although I’ve never worked with anything but quality products, when my daughters became vegans, that really broadened my horizons. The way I think about food has changed – for my daughters, but also for the climate. Of course I want to leave behind a better world for my children. What is remarkable is that it’s my own children who are showing me the way forward. A professional kitchen like mine serves as a showcase for my guests – everything that’s possible in terms of flavour is on display. I really love traditions. We celebrate everything at our house – we like to spread joy, and we want to do this on a deeper level too, for the planet. At Christmas, I’m certainly open to serving a butternut squash as a roast. As long as it’s delicious, and as long as it’s thrilling and dramatic – that is what makes it truly festive. You can use spices, mandarin oranges, and other citrus fruits to provide those traditional Christmas flavours.

In our restaurants, we often make dishes that would traditionally contain meat, like cassoulet, casseroles, ravioli, and lasagne, but then vegetarian. We replace the animal component with something plant-based. One challenge when making vegan dishes is how to make sure they have the same depth and richness as dishes based on animal ingredients. You want to serve dishes that are exciting, visually appealing, and expressive. Dishes good enough to win over carnivores – and for a humble pub like ours, that is no mean feat. I’ve been cooking professionally for thirty-five years now, and vegan cooking has provided me with a whole new range of possibilities – and I take even more pleasure in my work.

ANDREW COOKS: **VEGAN CHICKEN RISOTTO**

VEGAN CHICKEN RISOTTO WITH CRISPY YOUNG NETTLE LEAVES

4–5 servings (main dish) 1 hour and 40 minutes

30 g dried porcini mushrooms (boletus)
1¼ l vegetable stock
60 g blanched hazelnuts (filberts)
400 g fresh porcini mushrooms (boletus)
30 young nettle leaves
1 small onion
1 garlic clove
olive oil
1 tbsp fresh thyme leaves
freshly ground black pepper and salt
350 g risotto rice (Carnaroli)
75 g cold vegan margarine
2 vegan Chicken Breasts by The Vegetarian Butcher
small bunch (about 15 g) of flat parsley
2–3 tbsp aged Madeira

Pour the vegetable stock into a pan, add the dried mushrooms, and leave to soak for at least 1 hour.

In a small frying pan over medium-low heat, toast the hazelnuts until brown, stirring gently. Transfer to a plate and allow to cool.

Clean the fresh porcini mushrooms and cut them in half. Set aside 4 to 5 of the mushroom halves (one for each serving). Chop the rest of the mushrooms into pieces of 1 to 2 cm. Wash and dry the nettle leaves. Peel and finely chop the onion and garlic.

To make the risotto, bring the stock to a boil. In a large deep pan, heat a generous splash of olive oil over medium heat. Add the onion and fry until slightly browned. Add the garlic and thyme, and fry for another minute. Now turn up the heat and add the fresh porcini pieces along with a dash of pepper and salt. Stir-fry for 3 minutes. Then add the rice and stir-fry for 1 minute. Pour enough of the hot stock into the pan to just cover the rice. (If you'd like to add the soaked mushrooms from the stock, chop them first.)

Bring this mixture to a boil, turn down the heat, and stir until the rice has absorbed all of the stock. Then add 1 to 2 additional large ladlefuls of stock, and continue to stir until all of the stock has been absorbed. Repeat this process until the rice is cooked but still slightly firm – this will take about 20 minutes, and you might not need all the stock. Remove the pan from the heat, cut 50 grams of the cold margarine into cubes, and stir them into the risotto. Taste, and season with pepper and salt. Cover the pan with a lid, and allow the risotto to stand for 3 to 5 minutes.

About 10 minutes before the risotto is ready, fry the fresh porcini mushroom halves and prepare the crispy young nettle leaves. Heat 25 grams of margarine and a splash of olive oil in a frying pan over medium heat, and fry the halved porcini mushrooms for 3 to 4 minutes, turning regularly. In another frying pan, heat a layer of olive oil until hot and fry the nettle leaves until crispy, 4 to 5 at a time. Drain on kitchen paper, and sprinkle with salt.

Now cut each Chicken Breast into 6 large pieces. In a casserole over medium heat, heat a generous splash of oil and fry the Chicken Breast chunks until lightly browned. Stir into the risotto.

Coarsely chop the parsley, and stir into the risotto.

Spoon the risotto onto 4 or 5 warm plates. Sprinkle with the madeira and the hazelnuts, and add a bit more ground pepper. Top with the porcini mushroom halves and crispy nettle leaves.

2 servings (main dish) 25 minutes

TAGLIATELLE WITH VEGETARIAN MEATBALLS IN CREAMY MUSHROOM SAUCE

150 g tagliatelle
1 pack (170 g) vegetarian Meatballs by The Vegetarian Butcher
250 g white mushrooms
1 tbsp olive oil
100 ml vegan cooking cream
½ vegetable stock cube
6 tbsp vegan mayonnaise
freshly ground black pepper and salt
4 sprigs of flat-leaf parsley

Cook the tagliatelle until just tender according to the packet instructions. Drain, saving the cooking water.

Meanwhile, cut the Meatballs in half or into quarters. Clean the mushrooms, then chop into small pieces. Heat the olive oil in a large frying pan and stir-fry the Meatballs with the mushrooms over medium heat until browned. Remove the pan from the heat.

Add a generous splash (about 75 millilitre) of the cooking water to the Meatballs and mushrooms in the pan. Pour in the cooking cream. Move the Meatballs and mushrooms to one side of the pan. Crumble the ½ stock cube into the liquid and stir. Shake the pan back and forth a few times and bring the liquid to a boil. Cook for 2 minutes.

Remove the pan from the heat. Move the Meatballs and mushrooms to one side again and stir the mayonnaise into the sauce. Taste, and season with pepper and salt if desired. Stir in the tagliatelle, and heat until everything is warmed through.

Coarsely chop the parsley. Divide the tagliatelle over 2 plates and sprinkle with the parsley.

Tip: This recipe is also luscious made with Chicken Chunks.

Where does the tagliatelle go to dance? The meatball, of course. This tagliatelle with vegetarian Meatballs in creamy mushroom sauce is one smooth plan. A favourite of young and old alike.

4 servings (main dish) 25 minutes

SWEET-AND-SOUR VEGAN CHICKEN CHUNKS

1 garlic clove
1 onion
a piece (about 25 g) of fresh ginger
1 red and 1 yellow (bell) pepper
4 spring onions
sunflower oil
2 packs (160 g each) vegan Chicken Chunks by The Vegetarian Butcher
200 g ripe pineapple, cut into chunks
300 ml pineapple or orange juice
2 tbsp soy sauce
½–1 tbsp white wine vinegar
1–2 tbsp light brown sugar
4 tbsp tomato ketchup
a few drops of hot sauce
2–3 tbsp cornflour

Also needed: wok

Peel the garlic and onion. Finely chop the garlic. Slice the onion into half-moons. Peel and mince the ginger. Cut the peppers in half, remove the seeds and membrane, and cut into chunks. Slice the spring onions into pieces diagonally, keeping the green and the white pieces separate.

Heat a splash of sunflower oil in a wok over high heat. Stir-fry the onion, pepper, and the white of the spring onions for 3 minutes. Then add the Chicken Chunks, ginger, garlic, the green of the spring onions, and the pineapple and stir-fry for 2 minutes.

Add the fruit juice, the soy sauce, 1½ teaspoons white wine vinegar, 1 tablespoon light brown sugar, and the tomato ketchup and bring to a boil. Taste, and add hot sauce and more vinegar and sugar if desired.

Mix 1 tablespoon cornflour with 1 tablespoon cold water to form a smooth paste, then add to the pan while stirring and cook briefly until thickened. If the sauce isn't thick enough, make a paste with the remaining 2 tablespoons cornflour and 2 tablespoons cold water and add to the sauce until it has reached the desired thickness.

Tip: Good served with white rice!

This beloved takeaway classic is second to none. And so easy to do, you'll be making it at home from now on. So make like a chicken and fly straight into the kitchen.

4 servings (lunch or main dish) 20 minutes

VEGAN BURGER GALORE

1 large ripe tomato
4 hamburger buns
4 vegan Raw Burgers by The Vegetarian Butcher
4 slices vegan cheese
4 tbsp vegan mayonnaise
2 tbsp tomato ketchup
a few drops of hot sauce
8 pickle slices (along with the liquid)
4–8 lettuce leaves

Cut the tomato into 4 thick slices, and cut open the buns. Toast the buns, cut side down, in a dry (grill) pan or on the griddle or barbecue.

Fry the Raw Burgers in a hot pan for a few minutes, turning, until brown on both sides (or grill them on a hot barbecue, griddle, or grill pan, or under the grill).

Place a slice of cheese on top of each Burger, and cover with a lid. If you're using a pan, add a tiny splash of water to the pan to help the cheese melt better.

Meanwhile, make the Burger sauce by mixing together the mayonnaise, ketchup, hot sauce, and a little pickle juice in a bowl.

On the buns, build the Burgers with lettuce, tomato, pickle, the fried Burger, and of course the Burger sauce (or another sauce of your choice).

Tip: You can also top the Burgers with fried onion rings or pepper.

A truly juicy burger deserves to be the centre of attention. We called this vegan Raw Burger 'Patty on the Back' for a reason: it is a true reward. So treat yourself! Grill or fry the vegan burgers and arrange with tomatoes, and sauces into an attractive 'build your own burger' at the table. That way, everyone can take pride in their work.

4–5 servings (main dish) 45 minutes + at least 1 hour for marinating

VEGAN DELHI-STYLE BUTTER CHICKEN

a piece (about 50 g) fresh ginger
2 garlic cloves
1 small green chilli pepper
½ tbsp dried or fresh kasuri methi (fenugreek leaves)
4 vegan Chicken Breasts by The Vegetarian Butcher
4 ripe beef tomatoes (or about 400 g tinned peeled tomatoes)
100 g raw cashews
100 g vegan margarine
1 tin (70 g) tomato paste
1 tbsp soft brown sugar
1 vegetable stock cube
100 ml oat-based cooking cream
3 tbsp garam masala (Indian spice powder blend)

Also needed: mortar and pestle or food processor; casserole (Dutch oven)

Peel and chop the ginger. Peel the garlic. Cut the green chilli pepper in half, remove the stem, seeds, and membranes, and chop. In the mortar or food processor, grind the ginger, garlic, green chilli pepper, and kasuri methi into a smooth paste.

Cut the Chicken Breasts into chunks of around 3 cm, mix the paste into the chunks, and allow them to marinate (at least 1 hour, but they're also delicious if you leave them to marinate overnight).

Chop the tomatoes. Grind the cashews with the tomatoes until very finely ground. (Or mince the tomatoes, saving the juice from the cutting board, and finely grind the cashews in the mortar.)

Melt the margarine in a casserole over medium heat, and fry the marinated Chicken Breast gently until lightly browned. Stir in the tomato paste and fry for another 2 minutes. Stir in the sugar. Add the finely ground cashews and tomatoes (including the juice). Crumble the stock cube into the pan and stir. Allow the mixture to reduce slowly, uncovered, until the sauce is thick. This will take about 20 minutes. Stir frequently. After the first 10 minutes of cooking, add the oat-based cooking cream and the garam masala. Serve with basmati rice or naan breads.

Tip: If you like, you can also add 2 cinnamon sticks along with the cashews and tomatoes (remove them from the pan before serving).

Murgh makhani, or butter chicken, is a North Indian mild and creamy curry that is eaten with basmati rice or naan bread. This vegan butter chicken is to die for – yet no sacrifices are involved. Here's to you, our meat-loving revolutionaries, changing the world one dish at a time.

masakane
SABATIER

GUINNESS

4-6 servings (main dish) 1 hour and 15 minutes

IRISH STEW WITH VEGAN MEATBALLS AND GUINNESS

1 ½ l vegetable stock (made with 4 stock cubes)
6 dried porcini mushrooms (boletus)
6 sprigs of thyme
500 g waxy potatoes
500 g floury potatoes
4 vegan Raw Burgers by The Vegetarian Butcher
2 leeks
3 onions
800 g (smallish) carrots
about 500 ml Guinness
1 tbsp light brown sugar
freshly ground black pepper
8 sprigs of flat-leaf parsley

In a casserole (Dutch oven) or other deep pan, bring the stock, the dried mushrooms and thyme to a boil. Cook gently over low heat for 10 minutes.

Meanwhile, peel both kinds of potatoes. Cut the small ones into 4 pieces and the large ones into 6. Shape the Raw Burgers into 20 balls. Cut the leeks into wide slices. Peel the onions and slice them into rings. Peel the carrots, and leave them whole.

After the stock has simmered for 10 minutes, add the Guinness and the sugar. Stir and bring to a boil.

Add the potatoes, carrots, onion rings, and a generous amount of pepper to the stock. Cook for 5 minutes. Add Burger balls and leeks to the pan. Bring just to a boil, cover the pan halfway with a lid, and simmer for around 20 minutes until done. If necessary, add another 500 millilitres of stock to the pan. Taste, and season with more pepper if desired.

Coarsely chop the parsley. Ladle the Irish stew into warm deep plates or bowls, remove the sprigs of thyme if you like, and sprinkle with the parsley.

Wonderful served with warm crusty bread.

Tip: Irish stew can also be made with pearl barley. First wash 100 grams of pearl barley and allow it to drain in a colander. Then add it to the stock along with the dried mushrooms and thyme.

The basic ingredients for a classic Irish stew vary from family to family: with or without Guinness, with or without barley, with or without leeks, with one or two kinds of potato. It all comes down to what you like best. What this stew does always contain are carrots and onions – and also definitely vegan meatballs from now on. Let's get the balls rolling!

4 servings (main dish) 25 minutes

PEARL COUSCOUS WITH VEGETARIAN MEATBALLS

50 g raisins
300 g pearl couscous
200 g carrots
2 onions
1 yellow (bell) pepper
1 ripe beef tomato
4 tbsp olive oil, plus extra
1 ½ tsp ras el hanout
200 ml vegetable stock
2 packs (170 g each) vegetarian Meatballs by The Vegetarian Butcher
freshly ground black pepper and salt
10 sprigs of fresh coriander (cilantro) or flat-leaf parsley

In a bowl, cover the raisins with hot water and allow them to swell for 5 to 10 minutes. Drain. Meanwhile, prepare the pearl couscous according to the packet instructions. Add the raisins to the couscous.

Peel the carrots and cut them crosswise into slices or lengthwise into quarters. Peel the onions and slice them into rings. Cut the pepper in half, remove the top, and slice into strips. Chop the tomato.

Heat the olive oil in a deep pan and stir-fry the carrot, onion, and pepper with the ras el hanout for 5 minutes. Add the tomato and fry for another 3 minutes. Pour in the vegetable stock and add the Meatballs. Cook gently over low heat for 5 minutes. Taste, and season with pepper and salt.

Meanwhile, coarsely chop the herbs. At the end of cooking, stir three-quarters of the chopped herbs into the pan. Spoon the couscous onto plates and top with the Meatball and vegetable mixture, and some of the stock. Drizzle with a little olive oil, and sprinkle with the rest of the chopped herbs.

Vegetarian meatballs and vegetables stewed in stock and served with couscous. Even more delicious if you add a little saffron. You can eat this with your hands like they do in Morocco, or use a spoon like we do. Either way, it's finger-licking good.

4 servings (main dish) 25 minutes

VEGAN CHICKEN CHUNKS AND NOODLES TERIYAKI

300 g rice noodles
1 red onion
1 red (bell) pepper
1–2 red chilli peppers
200 g sugar snap peas
1 small spring onion
2 splashes sunflower oil
150 ml teriyaki sauce
2 packs (160 g each) vegan Chicken Chunks by The Vegetarian Butcher
12 sprigs of chives or fresh coriander (cilantro)
2 tbsp toasted sesame seeds

Also needed: wok

Cook the noodles until done according to the packet instructions. Tip into a colander, rinse with cold water, and allow to drain. Peel the onion and cut into strips. Cut the pepper in half, remove the top, the seeds and membrane. Cut into strips. Remove the stem and seeds of 1 or 2 red chilli peppers and slice into thin rings. (The more chilli pepper you use, the hotter the dish will be.) Remove the tips from the sugar snaps (as you're doing this, also pull off the tough string that runs along the side of the pod). Slice the spring onion into rings.

Heat a splash of oil in a wok over high heat and stir-fry the onion, pepper, sugar snaps, and three-quarters of the chilli pepper for 5 minutes. Mix in the noodles and half of the teriyaki sauce. Keep warm over very low heat.

Heat a splash of oil in a large frying pan and stir-fry the Chicken Chunks for 3 to 4 minutes until lightly browned. Add the rest of the teriyaki sauce and heat for another 1 to 2 minutes.

Coarsely chop the chives or fresh coriander. Put the noodle mixture into bowls and top with the Chicken Chunks. Sprinkle with the sesame seeds, spring onion, chives or fresh coriander, and some of the remaining chilli pepper rings (or serve them separately).

Tip: This dish can also be made with our vegetarian Meatballs, which you can leave whole or cut into quarters.

Vegan Chicken Chunks with colourful vegetables in teriyaki sauce: this plant-based winner rules the roost! Delicious, and done in a flash.

BREAKFAST, BRUNCH, AND LUNCH

4 servings (lunch or brunch dish) about 20 minutes

PIADINA WITH FRIED VEGAN CHICKEN, TOMATO AND TRUFFLE MAYO

2 overripe tomatoes
2 vegan Chicken Breasts
by The Vegetarian Butcher
olive oil
1 tbsp fresh or dried Italian herbs
freshly ground black pepper and salt
4 thin Italian piadina flatbreads (or wraps)
6 tbsp vegan cream cheese
8 tbsp vegan truffle mayonnaise
handful of rucola

Also needed: 2 large frying pans

Cut the tomatoes into small pieces and the Chicken Breasts into thin slices.

Heat a splash of olive oil in a large frying pan over medium heat and stir-fry the Chicken Breast slices along with the tomato and Italian herbs with a little pepper and salt for 8 minutes.

Spread the piadina flatbreads with the cream cheese, and top one half of each piadina flatbread with the seasoned Chicken Breast-tomato mixture. Wipe out the frying pan.

Spoon the truffle mayonnaise over the Chicken Breast mixture, and sprinkle on the rucola. Fold the other half of the piadina over the side with the toppings.

Place the filled piadinas in the 2 frying pans (without any oil). Place them over medium heat and fry the piadinas for 2 to 3 minutes on each side.

Transfer to plates or wooden cutting boards and serve immediately.

Tip: You can use sun-dried tomato instead of overripe tomato. This is also delicious served with olives and artichoke hearts. The truffle mayonnaise can be replaced with saffron mayonnaise, which you can make yourself with vegan mayonnaise and a few threads of saffron.

What the cluck? This luscious Italian hot sandwich is made from a very thin pizza-like dough, which is folded in half before frying. Piadinas can be filled with whatever you like most. But this version will keep you flying right!

Scandinavian Open-faced Sandwiches with Vegan Chicken

Tea Sandwiches with Vegan Chicken

4 servings (breakfast, brunch, or lunch dish) 15 minutes

SCANDINAVIAN OPEN-FACED SANDWICHES WITH VEGAN CHICKEN

2 celery stalks
1 small red apple
¼ lemon
a pinch of curry powder, plus extra
6 tbsp vegan mayonnaise
freshly ground black pepper
25 g vegan margarine
1 pack (160 g) vegan Chicken Chunks by The Vegetarian Butcher
4 (oval) slices wholegrain bread
4–8 lettuce leaves
2 tbsp piccalilli

Slice the celery stalks into thin arches. Cut the apple in half and remove the core. Chop the apple and put in a bowl. Squeeze the lemon onto the apple pieces. Add the curry powder, 4 tablespoons mayonnaise, and the celery. Taste, and season the celery salad with pepper. Add a little more curry powder if desired.

Melt the margarine in a deep pan and allow it to brown slightly. Then add the Chicken Chunks, sprinkle with some curry powder, and stir-fry for 3 minutes.

Spread the bread slices with the rest of the mayonnaise. Top with the lettuce leaves, Chicken Chunks, and celery salad. Spoon a bit of piccalilli onto the sandwiches.

4 servings (tea sandwiches or lunch dish) 25 minutes

TEA SANDWICHES WITH VEGAN CHICKEN

25 g vegan margarine
2 vegan Chicken Breasts by The Vegetarian Butcher
1 small cucumber
freshly ground black pepper and salt
8 slices from a white square sandwich loaf (pullman loaf)
4 tbsp vegan mayonnaise
1 tray (about 20 g) garden cress

Heat the margarine in a small frying pan and fry the Chicken Breasts for 4 to 6 minutes until brown on both sides. Allow to cool slightly. Peel the cucumber and cut into thin slices. Place the slices side by side on a cutting board and sprinkle them with a little salt. Allow them to stand for 5 minutes, then pat them dry with kitchen paper or a clean tea towel.

Cut the slightly cooled Chicken Breasts into thin slices. Spread the bread slices with the mayonnaise. Top 4 slices of bread with the slices of cucumber and Chicken Breast. Sprinkle with a little pepper. Snip off the garden cress, and sprinkle it onto the sandwiches.

Then top with the other 4 slices of bread, mayonnaise side down. Cut off the crusts, and slice the sandwiches diagonally into 4 pieces. Arrange the sandwich triangles on a platter or small plates.

4 servings (brunch or lunch dish, or as an appetizer) 25 minutes

VOL-AU-VENTS WITH VEGAN CHICKEN CHUNK RAGOUT

6 spring onions
6 sprigs of tarragon or dill
1 pack (160 g) vegan Chicken Chunks by The Vegetarian Butcher
60 g vegan margarine
4 level tbsp flour
1 ½ tsp curry powder
½ tsp paprika (powder)
250 ml vegetable stock
50 ml dry white wine
100 ml vegan cooking cream
freshly ground black pepper and salt
4 vegan vol-au-vent cases

Preheat the oven to 180 °C. Slice the spring onions into rings. Keep the dark green rings separate from the light green and white rings. Finely chop the tarragon or dill. Cut the Chicken Chunks into slightly smaller pieces.

Melt half of the margarine in a deep pan and allow it to brown slightly. Add the Chicken Chunk pieces along with the light green and white spring onion rings and stir-fry for 3 minutes.

Remove the pan from the heat. Add the rest of the margarine to the pan and allow it to melt. Then stir the tarragon or dill, flour, curry and paprika into the Chicken Chunks. Return the pan to the heat. Over low heat, let the mixture simmer for 2 minutes, stirring, to allow the flour to partially cook. Then pour in half of the stock while stirring vigorously. Add the rest of the stock, the wine, and the cooking cream and keep stirring until there are no more lumps. Allow the ragout to cook gently for another 5 minutes. Taste, and season with a little pepper and salt.

Meanwhile, heat the vol-au-vent cases in the hot oven for 5 to 8 minutes. Place the cases on 4 plates and fill them with a generous amount of Chicken Chunk ragout. Sprinkle with the dark green spring onion rings.

Tip: Add a small spoonful of mustard or horse-radish cream to the ragout. Finely chopped chives or chervil are also a tasty addition.

Vol-au-vents with ragout add a festive touch to any celebration, such as Easter brunch or Christmas breakfast. If it were up to us, we would have this for brunch every weekend – reason enough to get up with the chickens!

'I think that the current interest in more plant-based menus is crucially important.'

James Goodyear began his career at the age of seventeen, when he went to work under acclaimed chef Raymond Blanc. Since then, he has worked in world-renowned restaurants both in Britain and abroad. In 2021, he was named head chef at Adam's, a Michelin-starred restaurant in Birmingham, England.

I've had classical French training, having gone to work in the kitchen of the great Raymond Blanc when I was seventeen. But I've also worked at Mugaritz** in the Basque Country and at Maeemo in Norway, which was awarded its third Michelin star during my time there. Fermentation, foraging, constantly sensing that connection with the natural environment – I experienced these things there, and I will always carry them with me.

I think that the current interest in more plant-based menus is crucially important. We have to rethink the way we see food right now so that there is something left for future generations. In our restaurant, I love to cook vegetarian and vegan menus, because all of my guests are entitled to an amazing experience. Personally, I find it both a pleasure and a challenge to come up with the best vegan dishes possible. My old teacher Raymond Blanc is famous for his creative use of vegetables, many of which come from his own gardens. So the importance of vegetables was drummed into me at an early age. I can think of many of Blanc's signature dishes that contained no animal products at all – one more reason I've always felt such deep respect for this man.

Food plays a traditional role in all cultures, and because these traditions have such deep roots, it's hard to change things quickly. Although I'd love to eat roast celeriac (celery root) at Christmas, getting everyone else on board with that is going to take time. We need to persevere and have patience. Chefs are very important to the transition to a more plant-based diet, because we can offer people new interpretations of those old traditions.

When I create a vegan dish, I often use the same flavours and techniques with the vegetables as I do with meat. For example, an excellent way to fix celeriac is to roast it until it has a nice crust, then pour on a beautiful sauce and carve it the same way you would a generous piece of meat.

I'd like to dedicate my recipe for this book to my friends and family, because there is no one I would rather eat this with than them.

JAMES COOKS: **KOREAN GOCHUJANG LETTUCE WRAPS WITH VEGAN CHICKEN**

KOREAN GOCHUJANG LETTUCE WRAPS WITH VEGAN CHICKEN

4 servings (snack) 1 ½ hours (including making the broth)

FOR THE BROTH
300 g carrots
2 small onions
3 garlic cloves
1 leek
1 tsp gochujang (spicy Korean chilli paste; Asian supermarket)
1 ½ tbsp sesame oil
2 tbsp honey
freshly ground black pepper and salt

FOR THE VEGAN CHICKEN
2 packs (160 g each) vegan Chicken Chunks or 4 vegan Chicken Breasts by The Vegetarian Butcher
1–2 tbsp gochujang

EXTRA INGREDIENTS FOR MAKING THE LETTUCE WRAPS AT THE TABLE
3 small red onions
50 ml rice vinegar
½ tsp salt
1 tsp sugar
3–4 tbsp sesame seeds
spicy mayonnaise (made from 100 g mayonnaise and 1 tbsp gochujang)
2 heads of lettuce
12 radishes
2 chilli peppers
½ cucumber
100 g kimchi (Asian supermarket)
8–12 shiso leaves (Asian supermarket)
100 g bean sprouts
small bunch coriander (cilantro)

Also needed: (Korean) tabletop grill or barbecue; rechaud for broth; heat-resistant bowl

For the stock: Do not peel the carrots, onion, and garlic! Cut the leek in half lengthwise, then wash and dry. Grill the carrots, onions, garlic, and leek on a hot tabletop grill or barbecue until well-roasted. Then place them in a deep pan, and add 1 ½ litres of water. Bring to a boil, and cook until the liquid has reduced to about 200 millilitres. Pour through a strainer into a heat-resistant bowl. The broth should have thickened slightly. Add the gochujang, sesame oil, and honey. Taste, and season with pepper and salt, and a little more gochujang if you like.

Meanwhile, prepare the Chicken Chunks or Chicken Breasts. Use the Chicken Chunks as they are, or slice the Chicken Breasts if you're using them. Marinate the Chunks or slices in 1 to 2 tablespoons of gochujang for about 30 minutes or longer.

Peel the red onions, and cut them into strips. Put the onion strips into a bowl and mix in the vinegar, salt, and sugar. Set aside for at least 30 minutes (or even a day or more).

Toast the sesame seeds in a dry frying pan over medium heat, stirring continually until golden brown, then transfer them to a small bowl. Prepare spicy mayonnaise by stirring the mayonnaise and gochujang together in a small bowl. Remove the leaves from the head of lettuce. Slice the radishes and red peppers. Slice the cucumber into long strips. Then put everything into bowls or on plates, including the broth, kimchi, shiso leaves, bean sprouts, and coriander, and place on the table. Light or preheat the (Korean) tabletop grill. Grill the Chicken Chunks or Chicken Breast slices for a couple of minutes on the tabletop grill until done. Let everyone assemble their own lettuce wraps using the ingredients they like best. Dip the lettuce wraps into the broth.

4 servings (brunch or lunch dish) 15 minutes

VEGAN CHICKEN CHUNK SALAD WITH CROUTONS, RASPBERRIES, AND WALNUT DRESSING

4 slices French bread or 2 slices of other bread
70 g vegan margarine
2 tbsp raspberry vinegar
1–2 tsp mustard
freshly ground black pepper and salt
8 tbsp walnut oil
1 tsp sugar (optional)
3 shallots
1 pack (160 g) vegan Chicken Chunks by The Vegetarian Butcher
150 g mixed salad greens
150 g raspberries

Cut the bread into chunks of around 2 by 2 cm. Melt 40 grams of the margarine in a large frying pan and stir-fry the bread for a few minutes until the croutons are golden brown.

In a large serving dish, mix the raspberry vinegar, the mustard, a little pepper, and a pinch of salt. Stir in the walnut oil. Taste the dressing, add a bit of sugar, a little more pepper, and salt if desired. Stir until the sugar is dissolved.

Peel the shallots and cut them into rings.

Melt the remaining margarine in a large frying pan and stir-fry the Chicken Chunks with the shallot rings for 3 minutes. Sprinkle with a little pepper.

Give the dressing another good stir, then add the salad greens and Chicken Chunks with shallot rings and toss. Divide over 4 plates and sprinkle with the raspberries and croutons.

***Tip:** The tastiest fruits are always those that are in season. Instead of the raspberries, you can use other soft fruits, as well as orange sections, grapes, and pieces of apple or pear.*

Oh là là! This classic salad is considered a unique regional dish all over France. Although the basic ingredients are the same no matter where you go, each region has hatched its own variation on this theme. This one is ours, and made for true chicken lovers.

6 servings (brunch or lunch dish, or as an appetizer) 25 minutes

CROSTINI WITH SAGE PESTO AND VEGAN CHICKEN CHUNKS

2 garlic cloves
1 large shallot
about 200 ml olive oil
100 g cashews or pine nuts
4 tbsp drained capers
2 bunches (about 30 g) flat-leaf parsley
10 g fresh sage leaves (or 10 sprigs of basil)
freshly ground black pepper and salt
1 ciabatta
1 pack (160 g) vegan Chicken Chunks by The Vegetarian Butcher

Also needed: hand blender with blending cup

Preheat the oven to 180 °C. Peel the garlic and shallot. Squeeze 1 garlic clove through a garlic press and mix with 6 tablespoons olive oil. Slice the shallot into rings.

Put the cashews or pine nuts in the blending cup of the hand blender along with half of the capers, the flat-leaf parsley, and sage leaves or basil sprigs. Process until coarse. Then add around 100 millilitres of olive oil a little bit at a time, blending after each addition. Taste, and season with pepper and salt as desired.

Slice the ciabatta into 12 slices. Brush both sides of the ciabatta with a little of the garlic oil. Place them on a baking sheet lined with baking paper and bake them in the hot oven for 10 to 15 minutes until crisp (they should still be nice and soft on the inside).

Meanwhile, heat a splash of olive oil in a large frying pan over medium heat and stir-fry the Chicken Chunks with the shallot rings and the remaining capers for 3 minutes. Sprinkle with a little pepper. Spread the crostini with the sage pesto and top with the Chicken Chunks and shallot rings.

Tip: You can fry fresh sage leaves in a thin layer of hot oil for a few seconds until crisp. Drain on kitchen paper, and garnish your crostini with the crispy leaves.

Crostini are slices of bread that have been rubbed with oil and herbs and then baked until crisp. We top ours with tender vegan Chicken Chunks and fresh pesto. A match made in hen-house heaven! They're also divine as a dinner party starter.

4 servings (lunch dish or as an appetizer) 1 hour and 20 minute

OLD-FASHIONED VEGAN CHICKEN CHUNK SOUP WITH VERMICELLI

2 onions
2 small leeks
1 large carrot (about 200 g)
4 celery stalks
1 large ripe beef tomato
4 tbsp sunflower oil
2 tsp curry powder
½ tsp ground allspice
freshly ground black pepper and salt
20 lovage leaves or 3 sprigs of rosemary
1 bunch (about 15 g) celery leaves
5 cloves
8 blades mace
1 pack (160 g) vegan Chicken Chunks by The Vegetarian Butcher
25 g vermicelli
3 tbsp soy sauce

Peel and finely chop the onion. Clean the vegetables. Slice the leeks into thin rings, the carrot into cubes, the celery stalks into arches, and the tomato into pieces.

Heat the sunflower oil in a deep soup pan and stir-fry the onion with half of the carrot over fairly high heat until slightly browned. Add half of the leek, half of the celery, all of the tomato, the curry powder, allspice, lots of pepper and a dash of salt and stir-fry for another 3 minutes. Add 1 ½ litres of cold water, the lovage or rosemary, almost all of the celery leaves (reserve 4 sprigs), the cloves, and mace. Bring to a boil, then allow to simmer over very low heat for 1 hour until about one-fifth of the liquid has evaporated. Taste. If necessary, allow the liquid to evaporate a little further for more flavour.

Meanwhile, tear the Chicken Chunks into strips.

Strain the soup into another pan. Add the Chicken Chunk strips, the remaining carrot, celery, leek, and the vermicelli to the soup and cook 10 minutes longer over medium heat. Stir regularly.

Finely chop the remaining sprigs of celery leaves and stir them into the soup along with the soy sauce. Taste, and season with pepper, salt, and a little more soy sauce if desired.

Tip: Delicious served for brunch or lunch along with slices of wholegrain bread thickly spread with plant-based butter.

This traditional chicken soup hack would make Grandma proud. Don't be fooled by the beef tomato – we promise it's vegan.

2–4 servings (brunch or lunch dish, or as an appetizer) 45 minutes

VEGAN CHICKEN CHUNKS WITH AVOCADO AND SPRING ONION

1 pack (160 g) vegan Chicken Chunks by The Vegetarian Butcher
1 organic lemon
2 tbsp chermoula (North African supermarket)*
5 tbsp olive oil
3 spring onions
1 carrot
3 sprigs of dill
2 tbsp vegan mayonnaise
freshly ground black pepper and salt
2 large ripe avocados (but still on the firm side)

* Chermoula, a Moroccan herb and spice paste, is available ready-made but it's also very easy to make yourself. Grind (in a mortar) or finely mince (with the chopper attachment of a hand blender) the following into a coarse paste: 15 g flat-leaf parsley, 15 g fresh coriander (cilantro), 3 garlic cloves, ½ red chilli pepper (without stem and seeds), 1 tsp ground cumin, ½ tsp cayenne pepper, ½ tsp paprika (powder), 6 tbsp olive oil, the grated zest of 1 organic lemon, and the juice of ½ a lemon.

Cut or tear the Chicken Chunks into strips, and put them in a bowl. Grate the zest of the lemon into the bowl. Cut the lemon in half; squeeze a few drops of juice from one of the halves onto the Chicken Chunks. Stir in the chermoula. Heat 2 tablespoons olive oil in a large frying pan over fairly high heat and stir-fry the seasoned Chicken Chunks for 3 to 4 minutes. Allow to cool on a large plate, turning regularly.

Cut the spring onions into thin rings and the carrot into short thin strips. Coarsely chop the dill.

Put the mayonnaise into a bowl. Squeeze half of the lemon into the bowl and very gradually stir in 3 tablespoons olive oil and 2 tablespoons cold water. Add three-quarters of the dill, a little pepper, and a pinch of salt.

Cut the avocados in half and remove the stones. Scoop the avocado flesh out of the peel and cut it into pieces. Squeeze a little lemon juice over the avocado. Put the avocado in a bowl and toss gently with the slightly cooled Chicken Chunks, three-quarters of the carrot, and three-quarters of the spring onions. Spoon over the dill-mayonnaise dressing and sprinkle with the remaining dill, carrot, and spring onion. Pile the salad back in the avocado shells.

Avocados are now part of every brunch buffet, and so this golden egg was quickly laid. Today's menu features tender vegan Chicken Chunks with creamy avocado and crunchy rings of spring onion! If you allow for half an avocado per person, you have an appetizer or an addition to an elaborate brunch. Allow for two halves per person, and you have a fine lunch.

4–6 servings (lunch dish) 1 hour and 15 minutes

POKE BOWL WITH VEGAN CHICKEN

250 g sushi rice
2 large juicy organic limes (or 3 medium)
50–75 ml soy sauce
3 tbsp rice or apple cider vinegar
1–3 tbsp icing sugar (powdered sugar)
2 tbsp sunflower oil
2 packs (160 g each) vegan Chicken Chunks by The Vegetarian Butcher
16–20 green mini asparagus
¼ cucumber
3 tbsp vegan mayonnaise
a few drops of hot sauce
4 tbsp spiced toasted coconut (such as Indonesian serundeng)
1 ripe (but still on the firm side) avocado
50 g baby spinach or lamb's lettuce
100 g ready-made seaweed salad (refrigerator section of supermarket)
100 g carrots, grated
2 tbsp crispy fried onions (ready-made)

Also needed: wok

Prepare the rice according to the packet instructions, or wash the rice until the water runs clear and allow it to stand for 1 hour. In a narrow high-sided pan, bring 375 millilitres of cold water to a boil along with the washed rice and a pinch of salt. Stir, then place a clean ironed tea towel over the top of the pan and cover with the lid. Fold the corners of the tea towel up and over the lid so they don't touch the stove-top. Allow the covered rice to cook gently over very low heat for 15 to 20 minutes until done.

Meanwhile, grate the zest of 1 to 2 limes into a bowl, then squeeze in the juice of the lime(s). Add 50 millilitres of soy sauce, the vinegar, and 1 tablespoon icing sugar. Mix well. Taste, and add a little more soy sauce and icing sugar if desired.

Spoon the hot cooked rice into a wide dish and mix with 3 tablespoons of the lime-soy dressing. Allow the rice to cool, stirring regularly.

Heat the sunflower oil in a wok over high heat and fry the Chicken Chunks for 3 to 4 minutes. Add the remaining lime-soy dressing. Bring nearly to a boil and allow the liquid to reduce for a few minutes until it is slightly syrupy while continuing to turn the Chicken Chunks regularly. Then turn off the heat at once and allow the Chicken Chunks to cool slightly.

Break off the woody bottoms of the asparagus spears. Cook them in lightly salted boiling water for 3 minutes. Drain, and rinse under cold running water.

Peel and dice the cucumber.

Mix the mayonnaise with a few drops of hot sauce and a few drops of lime juice. Stir in 1 tablespoon spiced toasted coconut.

Shortly before serving, cut the avocado lengthwise into 12 slices. Sprinkle with a little lime juice so the avocado doesn't turn brown.

Spoon the rice into large bowls. Arrange the other ingredients next to each other over the rice, and add the remaining reduced dressing, if desired. Serve at once.

4 servings (appetizer or lunch dish) 20 minutes

CAESAR SALAD WITH CRISPY VEGAN CHICKEN

2 slices crusty white bread with seeds
olive oil
1 garlic clove
100 g grated vegan Parmesan or a tasty cashew cheese
100 g vegan mayonnaise
3–4 drops hot red pepper sauce (such as Tabasco), plus extra
1 tsp vegan Worcestershire sauce, plus extra
1 small lemon
freshly ground black pepper and salt
1 head romaine lettuce (cos lettuce)
6 vegan Crispy Chicken Burgers by The Vegetarian Butcher
4 sprigs of flat-leaf parsley or basil
2 tbsp capers

To make the croutons, cut the bread into large pieces. Heat a splash of olive oil in a large frying pan over medium heat, add the bread pieces, and stir-fry until crisp and golden brown. Allow to drain on kitchen paper.

Peel the garlic clove and squeeze it through a garlic press into a small bowl. Add half of the cheese to the bowl. Add the mayonnaise, hot red pepper sauce, and Worcestershire sauce. Wash and dry the lemon, and grate the zest into the bowl. Cut the lemon in half and squeeze the juice of 1 of the halves into the bowl. Stir well. Taste the Caesar salad dressing and if desired, add more hot red pepper sauce, (2 to 3 teaspoons) Worcestershire sauce, lemon juice, and a little pepper and salt.

Wash and dry the lettuce. Tear the lettuce leaves into pieces, and put them in a serving dish or on 4 deep plates or wide bowls.

Heat a splash of olive oil in a large frying pan over medium heat and fry the Crispy Chicken Burgers for a few minutes until they're brown and crisp on both sides. Cut them into long, narrow strips.

Roughly chop the herbs. Distribute the herbs, Caesar dressing, croutons, and capers over the lettuce. Add the Crispy Chicken Burger strips to the middle of the salad. Sprinkle with the rest of the cheese.

Tip: This salad is also terrific if you add fresh or dried tomatoes or grilled green asparagus.

In this plant-based version of the traditional Caesar salad, we use our vegan Crispy Chicken Burgers: you know, the one with the most tender fillet with the crispiest crust, succulent as can be. This is also a real high-flyer made with grilled vegan Chicken Breast.

‘We work with The Vegetarian Butcher products because they taste the way they should.’

John Warrington is an artisanal butcher. He’s a real meat lover and also one of the first to carry The Vegetarian Butcher’s new meat. It all started with the smoker in his butcher shop Slagerij ’t Oude Ambacht in the Dutch city of The Hague.

I remember when Paul Bom, product developer at The Vegetarian Butcher, came here to smoke his first vegetarian bacon cubes. We have a big smoker oven at the shop, and I let him use it. That’s how I first came across The Vegetarian Butcher, and we were the first butcher shop to work with them. We still carry a selection of their products in our shop. Their vegetarian Meatballs, vegan Chicken Chunks, and vegan Raw Burgers provide really good vegetarian options in the barbecue platters we make during the summer. We’ve also got vegetarian meals, and we sometimes use The Vegetarian Butcher products in those. My colleagues said I was crazy, but you can’t fight this kind of development – it’s the way of the future.

I fully support The Vegetarian Butcher’s ambition to bring factory farming to an end. Those high-rise pig farms are out of the question – they can’t be allowed, whether you’re a butcher or not.

We work with The Vegetarian Butcher products because they taste the way they should – it really does resemble animal meat. Some vegetarians don’t like this new meat because they think it is too much like animal meat – imagine that. I’m a meat man to the core, although I have started eating less animal meat in recent years. For example, in the past I would have tended to go for a 400-gram steak, but nowadays that’s more likely to be 150 grams. One of my favourite dishes is pork tenderloin with kiwi sauce – I know, it sounds strange, but it’s incredibly delicious. You fry finely chopped onion along with cubes of firm kiwi fruit, and then make a sauce with reduced cream, soy sauce, and white wine. This could easily be made with the new plant-based meat, and although I am and always will be a traditional butcher, that’s something I would really look forward to eating!

JOHN COOKS: **SPANISH VEGETARIAN MEATBALLS D’OUDE AMBACHT**

4-6 servings (snack, tapas, or main dish) 60 minutes

SPANISH VEGETARIAN MEATBALLS D'OUDE AMBACHT

150 g small chestnut mushrooms (cremini)
1 onion
3 garlic cloves
1 carrot (about 70 g)
2 tbsp good-tasting stoned olives
1 red chilli pepper or ½ tsp chilli flakes
1 bunch (about 15 g) flat-leaf parsley
1 tsp dried oregano or 1 sprig of fresh oregano
1 tsp dried thyme or 1 sprig of fresh thyme
olive oil
1½ tsp smoked paprika (powder)
1 tin (70 g) tomato paste
1 bay leaf
1 tin (400 g) peeled tomatoes
1 tbsp agave syrup or sugar
freshly ground black pepper and salt
2 packs (170 g each) vegetarian Meatballs by The Vegetarian Butcher
3 tbsp capers in brine
2 tbsp macadamia nuts

Also needed: slicer or grater

Cut the chestnut mushrooms into 4 pieces. Peel and finely chop the onion and garlic. Slice the carrot. Cut the olives in half. Cut the red chilli pepper in half, remove the stem, seeds, and membranes, and finely chop. Remove the leaves from the parsley sprigs, and also from the sprigs of fresh oregano and thyme if using. Finely chop the leaves.

Heat a splash of olive oil in a large frying pan, add the mushrooms, and fry until nice and brown. Add the onion, carrot, garlic, and olives. Stir-fry for 2 to 3 minutes. Add the chilli pepper and paprika and fry for another 2 minutes. Stir in the tomato paste and fry over low heat for 1 minute longer. Add three-quarters of the parsley along with the oregano, thyme, bay leaf, the peeled tomatoes and juice, half a tin of water, and the agave syrup or sugar. Bring to a boil while stirring. Simmer the sauce over low heat for 30 to 35 minutes until it has thickened slightly. Taste, and season with pepper and salt. After 10 minutes, stir the Meatballs into the sauce and simmer for another 20 to 25 minutes. If it starts to get too dry, add a little water.

Meanwhile, dry the capers by pressing them between layers of kitchen paper. Heat a layer of olive oil in a small high-sided frying pan over fairly high heat, and 'deep-fry' the capers a spoonful at a time for 1 to 2 minutes until they are slightly dry and crisp. Allow them to drain in a sieve.

Then carefully slice or grate the macadamia nuts. This will look like aged cheese. You can also coarsely chop the nuts.

Serve the meatballs and sauce on an attractive platter, and garnish with the crispy capers, the rest of the parsley, and the grated macadamia nuts. Finally, drizzle a little olive oil over the Meatballs.

VEGAN CHICKEN CHUNKS AND WAFFLES

2–3 servings (brunch or lunch dish) 35 minutes

---

125 g flour
freshly ground black pepper and salt
¾ tsp baking powder
30 g demerara sugar (or turbinado sugar)
25 ml sparkling mineral water
125 ml almond milk
75 g cornflour
1 tbsp curry powder
100 g fresh white breadcrumbs or 50–75 g coarse dried breadcrumbs
1 pack (160 g) vegan Chicken Chunks by The Vegetarian Butcher
75 g vegan margarine
oil for deep-frying
handful of rucola

Also needed: waffle iron (stovetop or electric); brush for greasing the iron; deep fryer or other pan for deep-frying; kitchen thermometer

For the waffle batter, put the flour in a bowl and mix along with a generous pinch of salt, the baking powder, and the sugar. Stir in the mineral water and almond milk to make a thick batter (small lumps are fine). Prepare the Chicken Chunks: In a deep plate, mix 50 grams cornflour with 3 to 4 tablespoons water into a thick sticky paste with no lumps. Stir in the curry powder, a generous amount of pepper, and a pinch of salt. Sprinkle the fresh or dried breadcrumbs into a deep plate. Put the rest of the cornflour on a small plate. Coat the Chicken Chunks by first dipping them lightly in the dry cornflour, then in the cornflour paste, and finally in the fresh or dried breadcrumbs so that they are completely coated. Place them side by side on a plate or tray.

Melt the margarine, but don't allow it to brown. Heat your stovetop waffle iron, or switch an electric one on. With a brush, grease the waffle iron with melted margarine. Pour in enough batter so that the bottom of the waffle iron is three-quarters full. Close the iron and cook the waffles for a few minutes until light brown on both sides. Make the rest of the waffles in the same way.

Meanwhile, heat the oil to around 170 °C in a deep pan (use a kitchen thermometer) or deep fryer. Deep-fry the Chicken Chunks quickly (no more than 6 at a time) until light brown. Allow them to drain on kitchen paper.

Put the waffles onto plates, top with the deep-fried Chicken Chunks, and sprinkle with the rucola.

*** Salsa verde: Using a hand blender, blend 1 clove peeled garlic, 1 peeled shallot, 60 g mixed fresh herbs (such as chervil, dill, chives, flat-leaf parsley, and/or tarragon) and 3 tbsp yeast flakes until finely chopped. Grate in the zest of 1 organic lime. Then cut the lime in half and squeeze in the juice. With the hand blender running, very gradually add 8 tbsp olive oil and 6 tbsp cold water. Taste, and add salt, freshly ground black pepper, and hot sauce as desired.**

Chicken & waffles – soul food for the true chicken-lover. Traditionally, the chicken on these waffles would be covered in gravy, but with vegan Chicken Chunks, they're delicious just as they are. Add some mango salsa (see page 179) or salsa verde* and this dish soars to new heights.

2 servings (brunch or lunch dish) 20 minutes

VEGAN CHICKEN CHUNK CLUB SANDWICHES

1 plump courgette (zucchini)
freshly ground black pepper and salt
4 tsp mild curry powder
4 sprigs of tarragon and/or flat-leaf parsley
1 pack (160 g) vegan Chicken Chunks by The Vegetarian Butcher
10 semi-dried tomatoes in oil
6 slices seeded wholegrain bread
4 tbsp vegan mayonnaise
handful of mixed salad greens

Also needed: 4 wooden skewers; griddle, grill pan, or frying pan

Cut the courgette lengthwise into 6 thin slices. Sprinkle both sides with a little pepper, salt, and half of the curry powder. Coarsely chop the tarragon and/or the parsley. Mix the Chicken Chunks with 3 tablespoons oil from the tomatoes, the remaining curry powder, and the green herbs.

Heat the griddle or grill pan. Brush both sides of the courgette slices with a little oil from the tomatoes and grill them for a few minutes until browned on both sides. Remove them from the pan, then grill the Chicken Chunks for a few minutes, turning, until browned on both sides. Toast the bread slices, and spread with the mayonnaise (about 3 tablespoons). Divide the salad greens over 4 of the slices and top 2 of them with the Chicken Chunks. Top the other 2 bread slices with the tomatoes and courgette and divide the remaining mayonnaise over them. Stack the bread slices with Chicken Chunks on top of the ones with tomatoes and courgette, then add the remaining 2 slices (mayonnaise side down!). Place the club sandwiches on 2 wooden boards. Insert 2 skewers on opposite sides of each sandwich, leaving enough room between each skewer. Cut the club sandwiches in half between the skewers.

Tip: Serve the sandwiches with plain potato crisps.

This double-decker super-sandwich has two layers with different fillings, and the possibilities are endless. Different vegetables, different sauces... the sky's the limit. But there are two givens! A classic club sandwich is served with crisps (potato chips), and tender vegan Chicken Chunks play the leading role.

4–6 servings (brunch or lunch dish) 20 minutes

FLAMMKUCHEN WITH VEGAN CHICKEN CHUNKS AND CHERRY TOMATOES

300 g white flour, plus extra
freshly ground black pepper and salt
4 g dried yeast
4 tbsp sunflower oil, plus extra
2 packs (160 g each) vegan Chicken Chunks by The Vegetarian Butcher
150 g spinach
150 g cherry tomatoes
125 g red onions
200 g vegan mozzarella
200 ml oat-based crème fraiche
½ tsp smoked paprika (powder)

Also needed: wide pastry brush

Start with the dough: sift the flour into a bowl. Sprinkle a pinch of salt around the inside edge of the bowl and the yeast in the middle. Add 175 millilitres of lukewarm water and 3 tablespoons sunflower oil and mix. Feel the dough to make sure it's not too dry (it should be just barely sticky), and if necessary, add a tiny bit of water. Knead the dough for about 10 minutes until smooth and elastic. Cover the dough and allow to rise for 1 hour. Then knead again briefly.

Preheat the oven to 220 °C. Divide the dough into 4, 5, or 6 pieces and roll into balls. You can also make 1 large ball. On a floured worktop, roll the balls of dough into thin ovals or rounds. Transfer them to a baking sheet lined with baking paper.

Heat the remaining sunflower oil in a frying pan. Add the Chicken Chunks, sprinkle with a little pepper, and fry them on one side for a few minutes until crisp. Remove the Chunks from the pan. Stir-fry the spinach for 2 minutes until just wilted.

Meanwhile, cut the cherry tomatoes in half. Peel the onions and slice them into half-moons. Tear the mozzarella into pieces. Spread the dough with a thin layer of oat-based crème fraiche, staying 1 to 2 cm away from the edges.

Arrange the Chicken Chunks, spinach, cherry tomatoes, and mozzarella on top of the oat-based crème fraiche. Sprinkle with pepper and the paprika. Brush the edges with a little oil. Bake in the hot oven for 4 to 6 minutes until the edges are crisp and light brown.

Flammkuchen (tarte flambée, or 'flame tart') is an iconic dish that flew in from the Alsace region of France. Thin, crispy bread dough spread with oat-based crème fraiche and topped with juicy vegan Chicken Chunks, vegan mozzarella, and cherry tomatoes. We're all fired up!

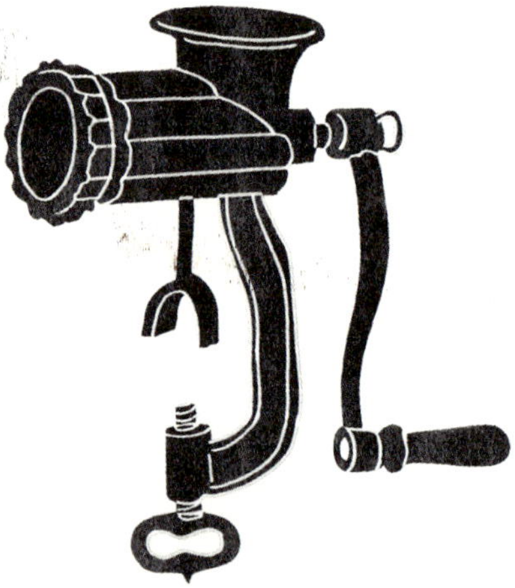

WEEK ENDS

4 servings (lunch or main dish) 35 minutes

VEGAN BURGER KOFTA WITH SWEET PEPPER SALAD

2 garlic cloves
small bunch of mint and/or flat-leaf parsley
4 vegan Raw Burgers by The Vegetarian Butcher
4 tbsp ready-made kofta seasonings
2 small red onions
freshly ground black pepper and salt
2 (bell) peppers (1 red and 1 yellow)
200 g vegan white cheese
100 g mixed olives
1 small lemon
olive oil

Also needed: 8 flat skewers; hot grill or barbecue

Peel the garlic cloves. Roughly chop the herbs. Put the Raw Burgers into a large bowl. Press the garlic into the bowl, add the kofta seasonings and 4 tablespoons of the chopped herbs. Mix well.

Divide the seasoned Burger into 12 pieces, and roll each piece into a long cylinder. Thread them onto the skewers and flatten them slightly. Put the kofta in the fridge until use.

Peel the onions, slice them into thin rings, and sprinkle them with a little salt. Remove the stems and seeds from the peppers and slice them into thin rings as well. Break the white cheese into pieces. In a bowl, mix the rings of onion and pepper with the cheese, the remaining fresh herbs, and the olives. Wash and dry the lemon, and finely grate the zest into the bowl. Cut the lemon in half. Add a generous splash of olive oil to the bowl, sprinkle the salad with a little pepper, and toss. Squeeze the lemon halves into the bowl and toss again. Allow the salad to stand for a bit to allow the flavours to develop.

Grill the kofta on the Grill the kofta on the barbecue or under the grill for about 6 to 8 minutes, turning regularly, until they are brown and cooked through. Spoon the salad onto a large platter or onto plates and top with the kofta.

Tip: Delicious served with pide (Turkish bread) or other bread grilled on the barbecue. This is even tastier if you drizzle the slices with a little olive oil before grilling.

On days off in Turkey, you'll see people everywhere having barbecues. Entire families will be busily lighting fires and preparing food. From carrier bags come salads, olives, loaves of bread, sauces, and also kofta, a wonderfully seasoned mince mixture that is often threaded onto flat skewers and grilled over hot coals on the spot. A delicious tradition – and one we don't want to keep from you.

4 servings (main dish) 15 minutes

VEGAN CHICKEN CHUNK MARSALA

1 garlic clove
2 shallots
40 g vegan margarine
2 packs (160 g each) vegan Chicken Chunks by The Vegetarian Butcher
2 tsp dried Italian herbs
75 ml sweet Marsala
150 ml vegetable stock
75 ml vegan cooking cream
a few sprigs of parsley or chives

Peel and finely chop the garlic and shallots. Melt the margarine in a large frying pan and when it begins to brown slightly, stir-fry the shallot with the garlic, Chicken Chunks, and Italian herbs for 5 minutes over medium heat until slightly browned.

Increase the heat to high, pour in the Marsala, and allow it to bubble for a moment. Add the stock and the cooking cream and heat for 5 minutes over fairly high heat to allow some of the liquid to evaporate so that the sauce thickens somewhat. Meanwhile, finely chop the parsley or chives.

Transfer the Chicken Chunks Marsala into a preheated serving dish or directly onto plates and sprinkle with the herbs. Good served with pasta and a fennel and carrot salad.

4 servings (main dish) 25 minutes

BARBECUED VEGAN CHICKEN BREAST WITH MAPLE-ROSEMARY GLAZE

1 bunch of rosemary (at least 6 sprigs)
1 bunch of thyme (at least 6 sprigs)
1 orange
10 tbsp maple syrup
freshly ground black pepper and salt
4 vegan Chicken Breasts by The Vegetarian Butcher
olive oil

Also needed: hot barbecue, preferably one you can close with a lid

Remove the needles and leaves from 2 sprigs of rosemary and 2 sprigs of thyme and coarsely chop. Wash and dry the orange, and grate the zest into a bowl. Cut the orange into 4 wedges and set aside. Add the chopped rosemary and thyme and the maple syrup to the bowl with the orange zest and stir together. Season with a little pepper and salt. Brush the Chicken Breasts with a little olive oil, and grill them on the hot barbecue for 2 minutes on each side. Close the lid if your barbecue has one, and grill them two more times for 2 minutes on each side; if your barbecue doesn't have a lid, grill them three more times for 2 minutes on each side.

Then brush the Chicken Breasts with the maple-rosemary glaze, tuck the remaining sprigs of herbs in between the Chicken Breasts, and grill them for another 2 minutes. Brush them with the glaze one more time. Serve on top of the sprigs of herbs, with the orange wedges on the side. Delicious served with noodle salad with spring onion and ginger.

4 servings (lunch or main dish) 25 minutes

TEX-MEX VEGAN BURGER

2 avocados
3 tomatoes
2 red chilli peppers
1 jalapeño pepper
2 organic limes
1 small red onion
1 tbsp fresh coriander leaves (cilantro)
freshly ground black pepper and salt
4 round bread rolls (burger buns)
1 tsp ground cumin
1 tsp chilli powder
2 tbsp sunflower oil
4 vegan Raw Burgers by The Vegetarian Butcher
4 slices vegan Cheddar cheese
2–3 tbsp vegan mayonnaise
8 Little Gem lettuce leaves

Also needed: barbecue, grill, griddle, or grill pan; 4 long, attractive skewers

Light the barbecue far enough in advance to allow the coals to get very hot; if you're using an grill, turn it to the highest setting to preheat.

Cut the avocados in half, remove the stones, and scoop out the flesh. Cut the avocado into pieces, and put them in a small bowl. Cut the tomatoes in half and dice. Put a third of the tomato in with the avocado, and the remaining two-thirds in another bowl.

Cut the red chilli pepper in half, remove the stem, seeds, and membranes, and finely chop. Slice the jalapeño into thin rings. Grate the zest of the limes into a small bowl, then cut the limes in half and squeeze in the juice. Peel and mince the red onion. Finely chop the fresh coriander.

Add half of the red chilli pepper and half of the lime mixture to the avocado-tomato mixture. Taste, and season the avocado salad with pepper and salt.

To make the pico de gallo, mix the tomato in the other bowl with the red onion, the remaining the lime mixture, jalapeño, and fresh coriander. Taste, and add chopped red chilli pepper and salt and pepper as desired.

Slice open the burger buns. In a small bowl, mix the cumin and the chilli powder with the sunflower oil, and rub this into both sides of the Raw Burgers. Grill the Burgers for about 5 minutes, turning, until they are hot and have grill marks. Top with the cheese and allow to melt briefly. Toast the buns in the pan (or on the barbecue or grill), cut side down, until brown.

Spread the bottoms of the buns with mayonnaise and top with some pico de gallo and lettuce. Then add the Burgers, and scoop a generous spoonful of avocado salad onto each one. Add the tops of the buns and insert the skewers.

This vegan Tex-Mex Raw Burger recipe from Dutch barbecue king Jord Althuizen brings you summer on a bun! Fresh avocado salad and pico de gallo – a spicy sauce made with tomatoes, onion, chilli peppers, and lime – give the grilled Burgers an exhilarating kick. *¡Viva la vida!*

4 servings (main dish) 30 minutes

OLIVE-STUFFED VEGAN MEATBALLS

1 onion
1 large carrot (about 75 g)
150 g stoned olives with herbs
4 vegan Raw Burgers by The Vegetarian Butcher
50 g vegan margarine
1 tbsp tomato paste
2 dried porcini mushrooms (boletus)
2 sprigs of thyme
½ glass (about 100 ml) red wine
200 ml vegetable stock

Also needed: casserole (Dutch oven)

Peel and finely chop the onion. Coarsely chop the carrot (no need to peel). Cut the olives in half. Cut the Raw Burgers in half. Roll the halves into balls and flatten them into discs. Put 3 or 4 olive halves in the middle of each disc. Fold the edges of the disc over the olives to close, and press firmly into balls.

Melt the margarine in a casserole. When the margarine starts to brown slightly, fry the meatballs over medium heat for a few minutes until browned all over. Remove the meatballs from the pan.

Add the onion, carrot, and the remaining olives to the fat in the pan and stir-fry for 3 to 4 minutes until the onions start to brown. Stir in the tomato paste and fry 1 minute more.

Add the dried porcini mushrooms (don't soak them in advance!). Remove the thyme leaves from the stems over the pan. Increase the heat to high, pour in the wine, and let it bubble for a moment. Add the stock and bring to a boil.

Return the meatballs to the pan and simmer with the lid half covering the pan for 15 minutes until done, turning occasionally. Divide the meatballs over 4 plates.

Delicious served with boiled or mashed potatoes and green beans, or with bulgur and ratatouille for a more Mediterranean touch.

Tip: The olives in this dish provide a flavourful surprise, but you can replace them with sun-dried tomatoes if you like.

The versatility of our vegan Raw Burger shines in this recipe. Broaden your culinary horizons and give these meatballs your own special twist.

‘We also make lots of vegetarian dishes in our home kitchen, because this makes Thérèse very happy.’

Chef Jonnie Boer and his wife Thérèse run De Librije, their renowned restaurant in the Dutch city of Zwolle. In 2004, they were the second restaurant in Dutch history to be awarded a third Michelin star, which they have to this day.

The most wonderful vegetarian dish we ever ate was actually an entire menu. This was at Alain Ducasse's restaurant in Paris – a real tour de force. If we were asked to name our own best vegetable dish, that would have to be the cauliflower with Madras curry. All the flavours really shine. Yes, that one remains a favourite.

Although we notice that people are choosing to eat vegetarian more often, our guests at De Librije still tend to go for meat or fish. So we believe in the power of the combination, and love to alternate between dishes with meat or fish and those that are plant-based. Right now we have lots of vegetable dishes. Alongside this, our guests have been able to order a ten-course vegetarian menu for years now, and it's a joy to create variations on this theme. We also make lots of vegetarian dishes in our home kitchen, because this makes Thérèse very happy. For us, the most important thing is always flavour. And I think that what's true in our kitchen is also true for sectors like the huge snack industry: as soon as a snack that contains no meat tastes the same as one that does, you've got yourself a worthy successor. Although we believe that plant-based dishes will continue to play an important role in fine dining, it's not always easy to get people to move towards the restaurant's vegetarian option. People simply have their preferences. For a long time, though, we've been working at getting our guests to choose for the vegetarian menu – so we are something of a pioneer in this way. We applaud The Vegetarian Butcher's ambition to bring factory farming to an end. And for us it's a beautiful challenge to continue to work with vegetables as much as we can, as long as they are grown sustainably. For the recipe in this cookbook, we took our inspiration from the ambiance of our restaurant Bar Senang and a wonderfully spicy dish made with vegan Chicken Chunks, lemongrass, and jeruk purut (makrut lime) leaves.

For us, the bottom line is always flavour. And if we look at the many good plant-based options that are already available, we feel that this market will only continue to grow in future.

JONNIE AND THÉRÈSE COOK: **CHICKEN CHUNKS MASAK LOMBOK**

4 servings (main dish) 40 minutes (best made 1 day in advance)

VEGAN CHICKEN CHUNK MASAK LOMBOK

10 candlenuts (kemiri nuts, Asian supermarket)
8 shallots
4 lombok chilli peppers (red and/or green)
1 organic lime
1 lemongrass stalk
4 garlic cloves
2 tsp tamarind pulp (Asian supermarket)
1 ½ tsp soft brown sugar
groundnut (peanut) or sunflower oil
50 g vegan margarine
2 packs (160 g each) vegan Chicken Chunks by The Vegetarian Butcher
1 ½ tbsp Indonesian soto spice blend or currypowder
4 jeruk purut leaves (makrut lime leaves, Asian supermarket)
6 tbsp sweet soy sauce (such as Indonesian kecap manis, or thick Chinese sweet soy sauce)
4 banana leaf wrappers (Asian supermarket)

Also needed: mortar and pestle (or cobek, Indonesian mortar) or food chopper; wok or large frying pan

Preheat the oven to 160 °C. Put the candlenuts in a baking tin and bake them in the hot oven for 15 minutes. Allow to cool.

Peel and finely chop the shallots. Cut the chilli peppers in half, remove the stems and finely chop (remove the seeds if you would like it to be less hot). Grate the zest of the lime, and cut the lime into wedges. Remove the hard, dry outer layers from the lemongrass stalk. Cut the tender 'heart' of the stalk into pieces. (Although you will add the dry pieces to the dish for flavour, you need to remove them again later because you can't eat them.) Crush the garlic cloves with the flat side of a chef's knife and peel them. Put the soft lemongrass hearts into a mortar along with the garlic and candlenuts, and grind them into a paste (or mince them finely in a food chopper).

In a small bowl, stir together the tamarind pulp, brown sugar, and 25 millilitres (about 2 table-spoons) of water to make a thick 'syrup'.

In a wok or large frying pan, heat a generous splash (about 75 millilitres) of oil together with the margarine. Stir-fry the finely chopped lombok chilli peppers, hard pieces of lemongrass, shallot, and lime zest for 3 minutes over medium heat. Do not allow to brown – if necessary, turn down the heat a bit.Then add the Chicken Chunks, candlenut paste, soto spices, and jeruk purut leaves to the chilli pepper mixture in the pan. Stir-fry everything for 5 minutes. Add the tamarind syrup and sweet soy sauce. Stir-fry the Chicken Chunks for another 5 minutes until golden brown.
Taste, and add a little more soy sauce and tamarind syrup if desired. You can eat the Chicken Chunks Masak Lombok immediately, but it's much more delicious if you let the flavours develop overnight! Remove the hard pieces of lemongrass before you eat. Serve on banana leaf wrappers along with the lime wedges.

Tip: Delicious served with steamed white rice or 'lontong'!

4 servings (main dish) 40 minutes

SAVOURY VEGAN CHICKEN CHUNK STRUDEL

1 large onion
6 celery stalks
1 organic lemon
2 sweet-tart apples
1 bunch (about 15 g) mixed Italian herbs
90 g vegan margarine
2 packs (160 g each) vegan Chicken Chunks by The Vegetarian Butcher
freshly ground black pepper and salt
12 filo dough sheets (about 375 g, freezer section, thawed)

Also needed: wok; wide pastry brush

Preheat the oven to 180 °C. Peel the onion and slice into thin rings. Cut the celery stalks into thin arches. Grate the lemon zest into a bowl. Then cut the lemon in half and squeeze the juice of both halves into the bowl. Cut the apples in half, remove the core, and cut into pieces. Add the pieces to the bowl with the lemon juice and toss. Remove the leaves from the sprigs of herbs and coarsely chop.

Melt 50 grams margarine in a large wok. When it starts to brown, stir-fry the onion with the celery over medium heat for 3 to 4 minutes until they brown and begin to soften. Add the apple and stir-fry 3 minutes longer. Add the Chicken Chunks and stir-fry for another 3 minutes. Taste, and season with pepper and salt.

Melt the remaining margarine in a saucepan, but don't allow it to brown.

Make the 4 strudels: When you're ready to assemble the strudels, remove the filo dough from its wrapper. Place 4 sheets of filo side by side on the worktop and brush them lightly with melted margarine. Top each of these with another filo sheet and brush with margarine. Then top each one with a third sheet, so that you have used all 12 sheets.

Spoon the Chicken Chunk mixture over the entire width of the bottom of the filo dough stacks, but stay a bit away from the edges. Roll up the dough around the filling and place the strudels on a baking sheet lined with baking paper. Brush with melted margarine and bake them in the hot oven for 10 to 15 minutes until light brown.

Tip: These strudels are made with filo dough. Filo dough is very easy to use but dries out quickly, so cover it with a cloth as you work. You can use fennel or pointed cabbage (sweetheart cabbage) instead of the celery.

Ah, savoury strudel from Austria... The sweet version made with apples is universally known and loved, but this savoury version made with celery, apple, and crispy vegan Chicken Chunks will win the hearts of many, from vegans to carnivores!

4 servings (main dish) 1 hour + cooling time

VEGAN ENGLISH BURGER AND MUSHROOM PIES

60 g dried porcini mushrooms (boletus)
1 large onion
2 garlic cloves
200 g fresh white mushrooms
50 g vegan margarine
4 vegan Raw Burgers by The Vegetarian Butcher
1 ½ tbsp herbes de Provence
freshly ground black pepper and salt
2 tbsp white flour
1 l vegetable stock (made with 2 stock cubes)
1 tbsp coarse French mustard
4 vegan puff pastry squares (about 12 ½ x 12 ½ cm; freezer section, thawed)

Also needed: 4 shallow individual baking dishes (about 300 ml capacity) with a wide rim

Put the dried mushrooms in a small bowl and add lukewarm water until they are just covered. Peel and finely chop the onion. Peel the garlic cloves and squeeze them through a garlic press. Clean the mushrooms and cut them into 4 pieces.

Melt the margarine in a large frying pan over medium heat and stir-fry the onion for 3 minutes. Meanwhile, squeeze the water out of the soaked mushrooms. Add the fresh mushrooms and the soaked dried mushrooms to the onion in the pan and stir-fry for another 2 minutes. Add the Raw Burgers and break into pieces with a wooden spatula. Sprinkle in the herbes de Provence and a little pepper, and fry for about 4 minutes until browned. Stir in the flour, fry for 1 minute more, and continue to stir as you very gradually add the stock. Bring to a boil and allow to cook gently over fairly low heat for 5 minutes. Stir in the mustard. Taste, and season with a little more pepper and salt if desired. Allow to cool.

Divide the mince-mushroom mixture over the 4 individual baking dishes. Cut a strip of about 1 cm from all sides of every puff pastry square. Moisten the wide rims of the baking dishes with a tiny bit of cold water, and place these puff pastry strips on top of the rims. Then moisten the strips with a tiny bit of cold water, and top with the puff pastry squares to cover the baking dishes. Seal the edges of the pastry by pressing down firmly on the rims of the baking dishes with a fork. Cut away any excess pastry on all sides of the dishes. With the tip of a knife, make a small hole in the middle of each pastry top to allow the steam to escape. Put the baking dishes in the fridge until use.

Forty-five minutes before you would like to eat, preheat the oven to 180 °C. Bake the pies in the preheated oven for about 30 minutes until golden brown.

Delicious served with mashed potatoes and green beans.

Tip: You can decorate the mini pies with the pastry scraps. Cut out shapes or strips from the scraps, and attach them to the pastry tops with a tiny bit of cold water.

SACRIFICE NOTHING

5–6 servings (lunch or main dish) 1 hour and 20 minutes

STUFFED PUMPKIN WITH VEGAN MEATBALLS, CELERY, AND BULGUR

1 orange pumpkin (about 2 kg)
4 vegan Raw Burgers by The Vegetarian Butcher
2 large ripe tomatoes
3 celery stalks
2 bunches spring onions (around 10 in total)
3 garlic cloves
1 bunch (about 20 g) fresh Italian herbs
200 g vegan white cheese
olive oil
150 g semi-dried tomatoes on oil
150 g bulgur
freshly ground black pepper
500 ml vegetable stock (made with 1 stock cube)

Preheat the oven to 190 °C.

Slice a 3-cm cap off the top of the pumpkin, then scoop out the seeds and strings.

Shape the Raw Burgers into 20 small balls.

Cut the tomatoes into pieces, the celery stalks into thin arches, and the spring onion into wide slices. Keep the white and light green spring onion slices separate from the dark green ones. Peel and finely chop the garlic. Remove the leaves from the sprigs of herbs and finely chop. Break the white cheese into pieces and place in a small bowl.

Heat a splash of olive oil in a large frying pan over medium heat and fry the meatballs for a few minutes until browned all over. Stir frequently. Remove the meatballs from the pan and fry the white and light green spring onion slices along with the celery and garlic for 2 minutes. Stir in the tomato pieces, meatballs, Italian herbs, semi-dried tomatoes, bulgur, and a little pepper.

Fill the pumpkin with this meatball mixture. Slowly pour in around three-quarters of the stock. Place the pumpkin on a baking sheet with the lid to one side, put it into the hot oven, and bake for around 55 minutes until done. After about 40 minutes, add the rest of the stock.

Slice the stuffed pumpkin into wedges, transfer them to warm plates, and sprinkle with the white cheese and the dark green spring onion rings.

Whether for a lavish Sunday lunch, a dinner party with friends, or at Halloween or Christmas, this stuffed pumpkin with meatballs means your guests will have nothing to beef about. Simply divine!

4 servings (snack, appetizer, or main dish) 1 hour and 45 minutes

VEGAN CHICKEN CHUNK SATAY

2 garlic cloves
6 tbsp sweet soy sauce (such as Indonesian kecap manis, or thick Chinese sweet soy sauce)
1 tbsp agave syrup
2 tbsp ground coriander
2 tbsp ground cumin
2 packs (160 g each) vegan Chicken Chunks by The Vegetarian Butcher
1 red chilli pepper
1 shallot
1 garlic clove
1 lemongrass stalk
a piece (about 25 g) of fresh ginger
2 tbsp sunflower oil
4 jeruk purut leaves (makrut lime leaves; fresh or frozen, Asian supermarket)
6 tbsp peanut butter
6 tbsp vegan barbecue sauce
freshly ground black pepper and salt
4 tbsp spiced toasted coconut (such as Indonesian serundeng)
4 handfuls cassava chips

Also needed: barbecue (ideally with a lid), griddle, or grill pan; 12 bamboo or wooden satay skewers (soaked in water for 30 minutes) or metal skewers

Start with the marinade: Peel and finely chop 1 garlic clove. Mix together with 4 tablespoons of the sweet soy sauce, the agave syrup, coriander, and cumin. Add the Chicken Chunks to the marinade, making sure they are completely covered, and allow to marinate in the fridge for about 1 hour.

Light the barbecue, or prepare a barbecue with a lid (and a thermostat) for direct grilling and heat to about 180 °C. The coals need to be red-hot. If you're using a griddle or grill pan, these do not need to be preheated.

Meanwhile, make the satay sauce: Cut the red chilli pepper in half, remove the stem, seeds, and membranes, and finely chop. Peel and finely chop the shallot and the remaining garlic. Cut the lemongrass stalk crosswise into 3 pieces and crush them with the flat side of a chef's knife or rolling pin. Peel and finely chop the ginger.

Heat the sunflower oil in a deep pan and fry the red chilli pepper, shallot, garlic, ginger, the lemongrass, and the jeruk purut leaves over fairly low heat for 3 to 4 minutes until somewhat translucent. Then stir in the remaining sweet soy sauce, the peanut butter, the barbecue sauce, and 60 millilitres of water. Stir well. If the sauce is very thick, add a little more water. Taste, and add pepper and salt if desired.

Thread the Chicken Chunks onto the satay skewers. Grill the skewers for 3 to 4 minutes on the grill grate until the Chicken Chunks are heated through and you can see some grill marks.

Serve on a platter along with the satay sauce (remove the lemongrass and jeruk purut leaves), spiced toasted coconut, and cassava chips.

4 servings (main dish) 30 minutes + cooling

VEGAN PATTIES STEW WITH CIDER AND ONION-APPLE RELISH

2 red onions
2 crisp sweet-tart Elstar or other apples
100 g cold vegan margarine
pinch of ground allspice
freshly ground black pepper and salt
2 tbsp soft brown sugar
500 ml cider (with or without alcohol)
3 sprigs of tarragon
4 vegan Raw Burgers by The Vegetarian Butcher
1 vegetable stock cube
2 cloves

Also needed: casserole (Dutch oven)

Peel the onions and slice them into thin rings. Peel and quarter the apples. Cut out the cores and cut into pieces. Heat half of the margarine in a frying pan over fairly low heat and stir-fry the onion rings for 3 minutes. Add the apples, allspice, pepper and salt and cook for another 3 minutes. Then sprinkle in 1 tablespoon brown sugar and pour in 100 millilitres of cider. Turn up the heat slightly and stir as you bring the mixture to a boil. Then lower the heat again and allow the liquid to cook gently and reduce for 15 to 20 minutes. Cook until around 3 tablespoons of liquid remain, the onions are nice and soft, and the apples have cooked down to a puree. Taste, and season with more pepper and salt if desired. Allow the onion-apple relish to cool.

Meanwhile, remove the leaves from the sprigs of tarragon and coarsely chop. Shape the Raw Burgers into 12 balls, then flatten them into patties.

Heat 25 grams margarine in a deep casserole over fairly high heat, and when this begins to brown, fry the patties for a few minutes until brown on both sides.

Pour in the remaining cider. Crumble the stock cube into the pan. Add the rest of the sugar, a little pepper, 2 cloves, and the tarragon. Bring just to a boil over high heat, then allow it to cook gently over fairly low heat for 10 minutes.

Remove the patties from the pan. Allow the liquid in the pan to reduce rapidly over high heat until about 100 millilitres remains. Add the rest of the margarine to the liquid and whisk until the margarine is melted and is incorporated into the sauce. Remove the cloves.

Place the patties on warm plates. Top each patty with a spoonful of onion-apple relish, and ladle the sauce around the patties.

Good served with mashed potatoes and Brussels sprouts.

Tip: You can easily replace the tarragon with other fresh herbs such as rosemary, thyme, or marjoram.

'Flavour has always been our top priority.'

Paul Bom comes originally from the hospitality industry, and over the past eleven years has been responsible for creating many new products at The Vegetarian Butcher. He even developed a vegetarian meatball that managed to fool a jury of master butchers.

I've been working for The Vegetarian Butcher for eleven years now, and it all began back in that first little butcher's shop that we opened in The Hague. I had a culinary background and thought: Why not?

To start with, my role in product development was to match flavours with the textures we were supplied with. Before long, though, I was involved at various levels of development. We went from buying the ingredients to making everything we sold, in collaboration with our partners. Of course, The Vegetarian Butcher is not a bakery, and we don't make the dough for our sausage rolls ourselves. We've joined forces with bigger and bigger players, and what I've said all along has come true: we are as big as the partner we collaborate with.

We're now busier than ever, but flavour has always been our top priority. In recent years I've been focusing on innovations. What this means is that once every six weeks I present newly developed products to our stakeholders. I'm given an ingredient and I get down to work. Can I use it to replicate a perfect piece of meat or fish? I find my inspiration in all kinds of places. It could be something I've seen in the supermarket or something I loved as a child, or a product I think should come onto the market.

The dish I'm making for this book is a combination of poke bowl and Mexican chilli. This recipe contains both our Chicken Chunks and our Raw Burger, and really demonstrates the versatility of the new meat. If I could dedicate my contribution to someone, it would have to be Jaap Korteweg. A remarkable man who, in the eleven years we've worked together, has shown complete faith in me and never once got angry, no matter how often things went wrong. I find that so amazing, and I certainly wouldn't have been able to do the same if I'd been in his shoes.

PAUL COOKS: **MEXICAN POKE BOWL WITH VEGAN BURGER AND VEGAN CHICKEN CHUNKS**

MEXICAN POKE BOWL WITH VEGAN BURGER AND VEGAN CHICKEN CHUNKS

FOR THE SUSHI RICE

250 g sushi rice
salt
2 tbsp white wine vinegar
1 tbsp agave syrup

FOR THE CHILLI SIN CARNE

1½ red onion (you can use the remaining half for the garnish)
2 garlic cloves
1 tomato
3 tbsp corn oil
2 Raw Burgers by The Vegetarian Butcher
1 tsp smoked paprika (powder)
1 tsp ground cumin
1 tsp dried oregano
½ tsp ground cinnamon
1 tin (70 g) tomato paste
1 tin (400 g) beans of your choice, or a mixture of beans
2 tbsp soy sauce
freshly ground black pepper and salt

FOR THE TOPPINGS

2 packs (160 g each) vegan Chicken Chunks by The Vegetarian Butcher
1 tbsp cornflour
6 tbsp corn oil
4 tbsp sweet chilli sauce
2 Romano peppers (sweet pointed peppers)
1 garlic clove
1½ limes
1 tin (150 g) corn
1 tsp dried oregano
½ tsp ground cumin
1 tbsp agave syrup
freshly ground black pepper and salt
125 g vegan sour cream
1 small red onion
1 large or 2 small ripe tomatoes
1 avocado
1 bag (about 200 g) tortilla crisps (tortilla chips)
1 bunch (about 15 g) fresh coriander (cilantro)

4–5 servings (lunch or main dish) 1 hour and 30 minutes

Prepare the sushi rice according to the packet instructions, or wash the rice until the water runs clear and let it soak for 1 hour. In a narrow high-sided pan, bring 375 millilitres of cold water to a boil along with the washed rice and a pinch of salt. Stir, then place a clean ironed tea towel over the pan and cover with the lid. Fold the corners of the tea towel up and over the lid so they don't touch the stovetop. Allow the covered rice to cook gently over very low heat for 15 to 20 minutes until done. Remove the pan from the heat. Allow the rice to stand for a few minutes, then spoon it onto a platter. Mix together the vinegar, agave syrup, and a little salt. Now gently stir this mixture into the rice. Stir the rice every 5 minutes until it has reached room temperature.

Make the chilli sin carne: peel and finely chop the onion and garlic. Dice the tomato. Heat the corn oil in a deep pan over medium heat, add the onion, and stir-fry for about 3 minutes. When the onion starts to brown, add the garlic, Raw Burgers, and spices. Break up the Burgers into crumbly pieces and fry for about 5 minutes until brown. Now stir in the tomato paste and fry 1 minute more. Drain the beans, and add to the pan along with the soy sauce and tomato, and stir together. Pour in 150 millilitres of water. Bring to a boil, cover the pan with a lid, and allow to simmer gently for 20 minutes, stirring frequently. Set aside.

Now prepare the other toppings. Mix the Chicken Chunks with the cornflour. Heat 4 tablespoons of the corn oil in a frying pan over medium heat, and fry the Chicken Chunks until they're crisp and well-browned (this works best if you fry them in plenty of oil). Add the chilli sauce, and allow to cook gently for a little longer. Set aside.

Cut the Romano peppers into pieces of about 2 cm. Peel the garlic, and squeeze through a garlic press into a bowl. Heat the remaining 2 tablespoons of corn oil in a frying pan over high heat, and fry the peppers until brown. Cut 1 lime in half, and squeeze one of the halves into the pan, then stir in the garlic, corn, oregano, cumin, and agave syrup. Taste, then season with pepper and salt as desired. Turn down the heat to low and heat for 3 minutes. Set aside.

Squeeze the other half of the lime into a bowl, and stir in the sour cream and a pinch of salt. Set aside.

Peel the onion, slice it into half-moons, and place in a bowl. Squeeze the remaining lime half over the onions. Mix well and allow to marinate briefly.

Cut the tomato in half, remove the seeds, and cut into thin slices. Peel the avocado and cut it in half. Remove the stone, and cut the avocado into thin slices.

Divide the rice over wide bowls or deep plates. Spoon the various toppings alongside each other onto the rice. Or place the rice on a large platter, add the toppings, and let everyone help themselves. Serve with the tortilla crisps and fresh coriander.

4 servings (lunch or main dish) 25 minutes

VEGAN BURGER BURRITOS WITH CORN AND HERB SALSA

1 garlic clove
1 bunch (about 15 g) flat-leaf parsley and/ or dill
1 tin (about 180 g) corn kernels
1 tsp coarsely ground smoked chipotle pepper or chilli flakes
1 organic lemon
75 ml sunflower oil
freshly ground black pepper and salt
4 vegan Raw Burgers by The Vegetarian Butcher
2 tsp Mexican spices*
4 large tortilla wraps
4–8 lettuce leaves

Also needed: hand blender with chopper attachment

* Would you like to make the Mexican spices yourself? Toast 2 tbsp cumin seed, 1 tbsp coriander seeds, and 1 tbsp black peppercorns in a dry frying pan over medium heat for 1 to 2 minutes until the cumin and coriander are somewhat darker but not black. Put this mixture into a mortar or the bottom of the chopper attachment and allow to cool. Then add 1 tsp coarse salt and grind or process until the mixture is finely ground. Stir in 3 tbsp smoked paprika (powder) along with ½ tsp cinnamon, 1 tsp dried oregano, 1 tsp dried coriander leaves, 1 tsp garlic powder, 1 tsp onion powder, and 2 tsp chilli flakes (use less if you want it less hot, and more if you want it even hotter). This spice mix will stay good for months if you keep it in a clean container or jar with a lid.

Peel the garlic. Finely chop the garlic and fresh herbs in the chopper attachment. Add half of the corn along with the chipotle pepper, and pulse until coarsely chopped.

Then grate the zest of the lemon into the chopper. Cut the lemon in half and squeeze in the juice of one of the halves. Add 50 millilitres of sunflower oil and 2 tablespoons cold water. Add the rest of the corn and pulse briefly. Taste the corn and herb salsa and season with pepper and salt.

Sprinkle both sides of the Raw Burgers with the Mexican spices. Heat a splash of sunflower oil in a large frying pan over medium heat and fry the Burgers for around 3 to 4 minutes until browned on both sides.

Meanwhile, heat the tortilla wraps in a dry frying pan for 2 minutes, turning to heat both sides. Place the wraps on a large wooden board and fold each wrap in half twice so that you end up with a quarter wrap. Tuck the lettuce leaves and Burgers into the wraps. Spoon a couple of spoons of salsa onto each burrito, and serve from the board or on plates. Serve with the rest of the corn and herb salsa.

Get your hands around these luscious tortilla wraps filled with crunchy salsa and spicy Mexican vegan Raw Burgers. Go on, dig in!

2 servings (lunch dish) 25 minutes

PULLED VEGAN CHICKEN ROLLS WITH BARBECUE SAUCE

2 tbsp apple cider vinegar
1 tbsp soft brown sugar
2 tsp mustard
1 tsp chilli powder
12 tbsp tomato ketchup
a few drops of Worcestershire sauce
1 large onion
1 garlic clove
sunflower oil
1 pack (160 g) vegan Chicken Chunks by The Vegetarian Butcher
freshly ground black pepper and salt
2 crusty vegan oval rolls

Make the barbecue sauce: In a bowl, mix the apple cider vinegar with the soft brown sugar and stir until the sugar is dissolved. Add the mustard, chilli powder, ketchup, and Worcestershire sauce and mix well.

Peel and finely chop the onion and garlic. Heat a splash of sunflower oil in large pan. Add the onion along with the garlic and Chicken Chunks and stir-fry over medium heat for 5 minutes. Add the barbecue sauce and a splash of water (about 5 tablespoons) and allow to simmer for 5 minutes. If the sauce gets too thick, add a little more water.

Transfer the Chicken Chunks and barbecue sauce to a dish and pull the Chunks into strips using 2 forks. Taste, and season with pepper and salt.

Cut open the rolls and fill them with the pulled Chicken Chunks and barbecue sauce.

Tip: Try serving them with pickled gherkins, pickled onions, or coleslaw.

There are so many ways our vegan Chicken Chunks can fly. This pulled meat is scrumptious on a crusty roll, and will be done hours ahead of the classic version. A top-notch hack!

4 servings (lunch or main dish) 50 minutes

GRILLED VEGETABLE SHEET PAN PIZZA WITH VEGETARIAN MEATBALLS

1 fairly small, thin courgette (zucchini)
1 red or yellow (bell) pepper
1 red onion
150 g green asparagus
olive oil
freshly ground black pepper and salt
1 roll (about 400 g) vegan pizza dough
1 bunch (about 15 g) mixed Italian herbs
3 roasted (bell) peppers (jar)
150 g semi-dried tomatoes in oil
4 tbsp stoned Kalamata olives
2 packs (170 g each) vegetarian Meatballs by The Vegetarian Butcher
1 bag (around 200 g) vegan grated mozzarella

Also needed: grill pan or griddle; hand blender with blending cup

Preheat the oven to between 220 °C and 240 °C.
Cut the courgette into long, thin slices and the peppers into thin rings. Peel the onion, cut in half, and slice into thin half-moons. Break off the woody part at the bottom of the asparagus spears. Put the vegetables into a large dish. Add a splash of olive oil and a pinch of salt and mix together.
Heat the grill pan or griddle until very hot, then cover with a single layer of the asparagus and sliced vegetables (next to each other, not on top of each other) and grill them for 2 to 3 minutes on each side. Remove from the grill and set aside while you grill the rest of the vegetables.

Line a baking sheet with baking paper and cover with the pizza dough, then press the dough out slightly to make it thinner. Bake the dough in the hot oven for 10 minutes.

Meanwhile, remove the leaves from the sprigs of herbs and coarsely chop.

Allow the roasted peppers (from the jar) to drain thoroughly. Then put them into the blending cup of the hand blender along with the semi-dried tomatoes and 3 tablespoons of the oil from the tomatoes, and blend into a thick sauce. Stir in half of the herbs.

After baking for 10 minutes, spread the tomato-pepper sauce onto the dough (leaving a clean margin at the edges). Arrange the vegetables, olives, and Meatballs on top of the sauce. Sprinkle with the remaining herbs and the mozzarella.

Bake the pizza for about 15 minutes more in the hot oven until the dough is cooked through and light brown, and the cheese has melted. Cut into 4 or 8 slices and serve immediately.

Pizza with balls – an all-around favourite! The vegetarian Meatballs stay nice and juicy in the oven when you sprinkle them with vegan cheese. With this pizza, you'll never strike out.

8–10 servings (main dish) 1 hour

MEGA VEGETARIAN MEATBALL-AND-VEGAN-CHICKEN CHUNK PAELLA

3 large onions
4 garlic cloves
3 red (bell) peppers
3 sachets (25 mg each) saffron
3 packs (170 g each) vegetarian Meatballs by The Vegetarian Butcher
3 packs (160 g each) vegan Chicken Chunks by The Vegetarian Butcher
2 tbsp smoked paprika (powder)
olive oil
freshly ground black pepper and salt
2 small organic oranges
800 g long-grain rice
3 l vegetable stock
400 g shelled peas (fresh, or thawed frozen peas)

Also needed: large paella pan (about 80 cm Ø)

Peel the onions and garlic. Slice the onions into half-moons. Finely chop the garlic. Slice the peppers into strips. In a small bowl, mix the saffron threads with 4 tablespoons lukewarm water. Cut the Meatballs into quarters. Put them into a bowl along with the Chicken Chunks and paprika and mix. Place the paella pan over a hot campfire with red-hot coals, or place the pan over the burners on the stovetop. The pan needs to be perfectly level. Heat a splash of olive oil in the pan and stir-fry the Meatballs and the Chicken Chunks for about 5 minutes until browned. Add the onion, garlic, and pepper, sprinkle with a little salt, and stir-fry them for a few minutes until they start to brown.

Grate the orange zest into the pan. Stir in the saffron (including the soaking liquid) and the dry rice. Make sure everything is evenly distributed. Pour in three-quarters of the stock. Sprinkle in a little pepper. Allow the rice to cook for 20 to 25 minutes until done. Do not stir! If the rice starts to dry out before it's cooked, add a little more stock.

When the rice is nearly done, distribute the peas over the pan, pressing them slightly into the rice. Allow to cook 5 to 10 minutes longer. Cut the oranges in half, and squeeze the juice from one of the halves over the paella. Cut the rest into wedges and serve with the paella.

Tip: If the paella is cooking too fast, move the pan further away from the fire (so, higher), and if it's not hot enough, move the pan closer to the fire (so, lower). At the beginning, start close to the fire (low) for the stir-frying.

This summery dish is ideal for serving to family and friends. One bite and you'll be back on the Spanish costa. Our hearty vegetarian Meatballs and juicy vegan Chicken Chunks are perfectly paired in this flamboyant flamenco of flavours.

4 servings (main dish) 30 minutes

TAJINE WITH VEGAN CHICKEN CHUNKS AND PRESERVED LEMON

1 preserved lemon (North African supermarket)
3 small red onions
8–10 (0.05 mg) saffron threads or a generous pinch of saffron powder
2 packs (160 g each) vegan Chicken Chunks by The Vegetarian Butcher
4 tbsp light olive oil
1 tbsp ras el hanout
2 tsp cumin seed
2 small cinnamon sticks
125 g large stoned green olives
250 ml hot vegetable stock
6-10 sprigs of flat-leaf parsley or fresh coriander leaves (cilantro)

Also needed: heat diffuser and a 4-person tajine (or, if you're using the oven, a casserole dish with a lid)

Cut the preserved lemon in half, scoop out the pulp (this will not be used), and cut the peel into 12 pieces. Peel the onions and cut each onion into 6 wedges. Put the saffron threads into a small bowl, add 2 tablespoons lukewarm water, and leave to soak for a few minutes. If you're using saffron powder, you don't need to soak this.

Put the Chicken Chunks into a bowl along with half of the olive oil, the ras el hanout, and the soaked saffron, including the soaking liquid (or add the saffron powder) and mix well.

Place a heat diffuser over a burner (stovetop) and set the tajine on the diffuser, or preheat the oven to 180 °C. Heat the remaining olive oil in the tajine (or frying pan, if you're using the oven) over fairly high heat. Add the cumin seed, stirring for 1 minute until the seeds start to pop. Add the cinnamon sticks and onions and fry for 5 minutes. Stir in the pieces of preserved lemon peel, olives, and seasoned Chicken Chunks. Fry for 3 minutes. (If you're using the oven, transfer the contents of the frying pan into a casserole dish with a lid.) Pour in the hot stock. Put the lid on the tajine and allow to cook gently over very low heat for 15 minutes, or put the covered casserole in the oven for 15 minutes.

Meanwhile, coarsely chop the parsley or fresh coriander. When the tajine is ready, sprinkle with the chopped herbs. Serve at once.

Tip: Good served with Moroccan bread.

The name tajine is used for both the dish itself and the earthenware pot the dish is cooked in. In a tajine, the food stews in the steam (condensation) that forms in the pot's conical or rounded lid. This not only cooks the food, it also keeps it juicy. And we love juicy meat – plant-based, of course! High time, then, for our vegan Chicken Chunks to make an appearance here.

4 servings (lunch or main dish) 1 hour and 10 minutes + cooling times in between

SPECIALLY SPICED VEGAN CORNISH PASTIES

1 large onion
2 garlic cloves
1 large potato
1 medium carrot
olive oil
2 vegan Raw Burgers by The Vegetarian Butcher
2 tbsp ras el hanout
2 tbsp white flour
500 ml vegetable stock (made with 1 stock cube)
freshly ground black pepper and salt
2 rolls savoury shortcrust pastry (pie dough),
6 sprigs of flat-leaf parsley and/or mint
150 g peas (cooked fresh peas or frozen)

Also needed: rolling pin

Peel and finely chop the onion and garlic. Peel the potato and carrot and cut them into cubes of around 1 ½ cm.

Heat a splash of olive oil in a large frying pan over fairly low heat and fry the onion for 3 minutes. Turn up the heat and add the potato, carrot, and garlic. Then add the Raw Burgers and break into pieces with a wooden spatula. Sprinkle in the ras el hanout, and fry for about 4 minutes until browned. Stir in the flour, fry for 1 minute more, and continue to stir as you very gradually add the stock. Bring to a boil and allow to simmer gently over fairly low heat for 15 to 20 minutes until the potato and carrot pieces are tender. Taste, and add pepper and salt if desired. Allow to cool.

Place 1 sheet of pastry on top of the other. Fold the pastry in half 4 times, then cut into 4 pieces and shape into 4 balls of approximately the same size. Flatten the balls slightly. On a floured worktop, roll them into 4 thin circles of around 20 cm in diameter. Chill them in the fridge until use.

Meanwhile, coarsely chop the parsley and/or mint. Add the peas and the chopped herbs to the filling for the pasties. Spoon the filling onto one half of each of the 4 pastry circles, staying back 2 cm from the edges. Moisten the edges of pastry around the filling with a tiny bit of water. Fold the other half of the pastry circles over the filling. Press down firmly on the edges with a fork, then fold the edges back slightly. Place the pasties on baking paper and put them back in the fridge until you're ready to bake them.

Preheat the oven to 180 °C. Transfer the Cornish pasties on the baking paper to a baking sheet and bake for around 30 minutes until golden brown.

Cornish pasties enjoy a long and rich history, and are an iconic British dish. This authentic Cornish pasty recipe showcases English comfort food at its very best!

mmmmmm
mmmmmm!

SNACK TIME

2 servings 20 minutes

VEGAN BURGER YAKITORI WITH SPRING ONION AND SEASONED MAPLE SYRUP

4 vegan Raw Burgers by The Vegetarian Butcher
sunflower oil
4 plump spring onions
6 tbsp maple syrup
4 tbsp soy sauce
1 ½ tbsp mirin (Japanese cooking wine) or white wine
1 ½ tsp freshly ground black pepper
50 g cashews

Also needed: barbecue, grill, griddle, or grill pan; 8 skewers (soaked in water for 30 minutes)

Light the barbecue or preheat the grill.

Cut each Raw Burger into 6 wedges. Heat a splash of sunflower oil in a large frying pan and fry the Burger wedges over medium heat for 3 minutes until very lightly browned. Turn once.

Cut the white of each of the spring onions into 3 pieces and the green into thin rings. Thread the skewers, alternating between Burger wedges and the white spring onion pieces. In a small bowl, stir together the maple syrup, soy sauce, mirin or wine, and pepper and mix well.

Coarsely chop the cashews.

Grill the yakitori on the barbecue, under the grill, on the griddle, or in the grill pan for 4 to 6 minutes, turning, until browned on both sides. Transfer to plates, and drizzle with the seasoned maple syrup and sprinkle with the spring onion rings and cashews.

Tip: You can also make this yakitori with our vegetarian Meatballs, which you first cut in half.

Yakitori (meat skewers) are popular at parties in Japan. Traditionally, yakitori is grilled over a charcoal fire, so break out the barbecue if you can and have a little fun.

16 servings   25 minutes

VEGAN BURGER BAOS WITH SESAME

3 spring onions
a piece (about 30 g) of fresh ginger
2 garlic cloves
4 tbsp sesame seeds
4 tbsp groundnut (peanut) or sunflower oil
4 vegan Raw Burgers by The Vegetarian Butcher
4 tbsp teriyaki wok sauce
16 baos (freezer section; Asian supermarket, or homemade*)
6 tbsp shredded cabbage and carrot mixed pickles (such as Indonesian acar campur) or seaweed salad (chuka wakame)

Also needed: pan with steamer baskets; mortar and pestle or hand blender with chopper attachment

* Sift 500 g fine white flour or bao flour into a bowl. Make a well in the middle of the flour, and into this well sprinkle 1½ tsp dried yeast, 2½ tbsp sugar, and 1½ tsp baking powder. Around the edge of (not in) the well, sprinkle ¾ tsp salt. Pour in 300 ml lukewarm water and mix well. Knead the dough on the worktop for 10 to 15 minutes until it is smooth and elastic. Grease the bowl with 1 tbsp sunflower oil. Place the dough in the bowl, cover with a damp cloth, and allow to rise in a fairly warm spot for 1 to 1½ hours. Then knead the dough for 3 minutes more, and divide into 16 pieces. Roll them into balls with floured hands. One by one, flatten a ball into an oval in the palm of your hand, brush lightly with oil, place a chopstick down the middle lengthwise, then fold loosely in half (don't press down). Remove the chopstick. Place the baos on squares of baking paper (7 x 7 cm). Brush them with a little oil, then cover them with a sheet of baking paper and then a cloth. Allow the baos to rise for another 30 minutes. Steam them according to the instructions in the recipe.

To steam the baos, shortly before serving heat a shallow layer of water in a pan with steamer baskets. Place the baos (on their squares of baking paper) side by side in the steamer baskets, leaving some space in between. Cover the steamer baskets with the lid, and steam the baos for about 15 minutes until done. Although it's handy to steam the baos in layers so you can do them all at once, you can also do this in batches.

Meanwhile, slice the spring onions into long, thin strips and place them in a container of ice water to allow them to curl. Peel the ginger and garlic, and grind or process them into a paste along with half of the sesame seeds. Mix in 4 tablespoons oil. Toast the remaining sesame seeds quickly (2 to 3 minutes) in a dry frying pan, stirring constantly, until golden brown. Transfer to a dish and set aside.

Cut each of the Raw Burgers into 4 pieces, and shape them into ovals. Coat them on both sides with the ginger-sesame mixture. Grill them (in a hot grill pan or on a griddle or barbecue) until lightly browned on both sides (about 6 minutes). Then brush them with the teriyaki sauce and grill for another ½ to 1 minute on both sides.

Pat the spring onion curls dry with kitchen paper. Slice open the hot baos and top with pickles or seaweed salad, the Burgers, and the spring onion. Sprinkle with the reserved sesame seeds, and serve the baos at once.

4 servings (snack or lunch dish) 45 minutes

VEGAN CHICKEN TIKKA SANDWICH

2 vegan Chicken Breasts by The Vegetarian Butcher
½–1 red chilli pepper
2 medium onions
1 large ripe beef tomato
50 g vegan margarine
about 60 g tikka masala paste (ready-made or homemade*)
1 tbsp tomato paste
75 ml vegan cooking cream
2 tbsp mango chutney
100 ml vegan coconut yoghurt
1 lime
4 naan breads (about 120 g each)
handful of fresh coriander (cilantro) or flat-leaf parsley

* To make homemade tikka masala paste: In the blending cup of a hand blender or the bowl of food processor, grind together 2 peeled cloves of garlic, 25 g peeled fresh ginger, ½ cleaned red chilli pepper (stem, seeds, and membranes removed), and the seeds of 2 cardamom pods along with 3 tbsp groundnut (peanut) oil, ½ tsp ground coriander, 1½ tsp ground cumin, ½ tsp turmeric powder, 1 tsp paprika (powder), and 2 tsp garam masala (Indian spice powder blend) into a smooth paste.

Cut the Chicken Breasts into 2-cm chunks. Cut off the top of the chilli pepper, scoop out the seeds and slice the pepper into thin rings. Peel and finely chop the onions. Cut the tomato into small pieces (save the juice!).

Heat the margarine in a small pan or casserole over medium heat, and stir-fry the onion and chilli pepper rings for 3 minutes. Add the tomato and Chicken Breast chunks and stir-fry for another 5 minutes. Add the tikka masala paste and the tomato paste and fry for 2 minutes more. Then add the juice from the tomatoes along with 150 millilitres of cold water, cover the pan, and allow the chicken tikka to simmer over very low heat for 10 to 15 minutes. Stir frequently.

Add the cream and allow to simmer 5 minutes more. At the end, stir in the mango chutney and half of the yoghurt and heat through. Cut the lime in half. Squeeze the lime halves into the pan and stir in the juice.

Heat the naan breads in a toaster, a hot frying pan over high heat (turning to heat both sides), or for around 5 minutes in a preheated 180 °C oven.

Cut them in half. Spoon the chicken tikka onto 4 of the naan halves, then spoon on the remaining yoghurt, sprinkle with a little fresh coriander or parsley, and top with the other halves.

Tip: Serve with lime wedges and more mango chutney if you like. To serve as a snack with drinks, cut the sandwiches into 8 pieces and insert a cocktail stick into each piece.

8 servings 20 minutes

FIVE-SPICE PANCAKES WITH VEGAN CHICKEN CHUNKS, CUCUMBER, AND HOISIN SAUCE

1 cucumber
4 spring onions
a piece (about 50 g) of fresh ginger
2 packs (160 g each) vegan Chicken Chunks by The Vegetarian Butcher
1 tbsp Chinese five-spice powder
5 tbsp sunflower oil
4 tbsp salty soy sauce
24 thin Chinese 'pancakes' (ready-made; Asian supermarket, or homemade*)
100–150 ml hoisin sauce

Also needed: pan with steamer baskets

* To make Chinese pancakes yourself: In a bowl, mix together 200 g sifted flour and a pinch of salt. Stir in 75 ml boiling water. Mix well and allow to rest for 5 minutes. Then add 50 ml cold water and knead until the dough is smooth and elastic. Turn out onto a floured worktop and shape into a thick roll (5 to 6 cm Ø). Cut the roll into 24 slices, and roll them out 2 mm thick. Steam them for 10 to 12 minutes until done.

Cut the cucumber and spring onion into long, thin strips (6 to 8 cm long x ½ cm wide). Place them on a plate or in a bowl.

Cut the ginger into very thin slivers, and the Chicken Chunks into thin strips. Mix with the five-spice powder and sunflower oil. (If you marinate the seasoned Chicken Chunk strips in this oil overnight in the fridge, they'll taste even better.) Stir-fry the Chicken Chunk strips with the ginger in a dry frying pan for 3 to 4 minutes until lightly browned. You can add another splash of sunflower oil to the pan if it gets too dry. Add the salty soy sauce and heat 2 minutes more, then transfer to a serving dish.

Place stacks of 6 pancakes on baking paper in the steamer baskets. Place the steamer basket on the pan over a layer of boiling water. Cover the steamer baskets with the lid, and steam the pancakes for a few minutes until hot.

Although it's handy to work in layers (multiple baskets) so you can steam all the pancakes at once, you can also do this in batches.

Stack the pancakes onto a plate, and place them on the table along with the Chicken Chunk strips, hoisin sauce, cucumber, and spring onion. Everyone can then assemble their own pancakes. Once you've added the fillings, roll them up and eat with your hands.

Pancakes filled with our vegan Chicken Chunk rendition of Peking duck. Sharpen those cleavers – this dish is the perfect hack of the Chinese classic.

12–14 spring rolls 30–35 minutes

VEGAN CHICKEN CHUNK SPRING ROLLS AND SPICY TOMATO SAUCE

75 g leek
75 g carrot
2 packs (160 g each) vegan Chicken Chunks by The Vegetarian Butcher
a piece (about 40 g) of fresh ginger
1 garlic clove
1 small red chilli pepper
oil for frying and deep-frying
1 ½ tsp curry powder
5 tbsp sweet soy sauce (such as Indonesian kecap manis, or thick Chinese sweet soy sauce)
100 g bean sprouts
freshly ground black pepper and salt
12–14 square spring roll wrappers (freezer section, thawed)
8 tbsp tomato ketchup
2–3 tbsp hot thick pepper sauce (such as sambal oelek)
a few drops of lemon or lime juice

Also needed: deep fryer or other pan for deep-frying; kitchen thermometer

Clean the leek and carrot. Cut the Chicken Chunks, leek, and carrot into long, thin strips (6 to 8 cm). Peel and grate the ginger. Peel and finely chop the garlic. Cut the chilli pepper in half, remove the stem, seeds, and membranes, and finely chop.

Heat a little oil in a wok or high-sided frying pan and stir-fry the Chicken Chunks along with the carrot, ginger, garlic, red chilli pepper, and curry powder over high heat for 3 minutes. Then add the leek, and stir-fry 1 minute more. Add the sweet soy sauce and stir-fry for another 2 minutes. Turn off the heat and stir in the bean sprouts. Season with pepper and salt.

Place the spring roll wrappers side by side on the worktop so that one corner of the wrappers is pointing at you. Spoon rows of Chicken Chunk filling just below the middle of the wrappers. Fold the bottom corner up over the filling, then fold in the side corners. Moisten the edges of the top corner with a little cold water, and roll up the spring roll (not too tightly). Place the spring rolls side by side and cover until needed.

Deep-fry the spring rolls in the oil (at around 170 °C; use a kitchen thermometer if you're deep-frying in an ordinary pan) for a few minutes until golden brown. Allow them to drain on kitchen paper. You can also bake the spring rolls in the oven. To do this, brush them first with a little oil and bake them on a baking sheet lined with baking paper for about 10 minutes at 220 °C.

Make the spicy tomato sauce. Mix the ketchup with the hot pepper sauce and the lemon or lime juice until smooth.

Freshly fried spring rolls filled with crispy vegan Chicken Chunks. Slightly spicy and bursting with flavour. These spring rolls are on a roll!

16 patties **20 minutes to 2 hours**

VEGAN JALAPEÑO PATTIES WITH MANGO SALSA

1 ripe mango
1 small red onion
10 sprigs of fresh coriander (cilantro) or mint
4–5 jalapeño peppers (green and red)
2 organic limes
1 tbsp ginger syrup (Asian supermarket, or use syrup from a jar of preserved ginger)
2 tbsp sunflower oil, plus extra
freshly ground black pepper and salt
4 vegan Raw Burgers by The Vegetarian Butcher

For the mango salsa, peel the mango, cut the flesh from the stone, then cut into pieces and put in a bowl. Peel the onion and slice into thin strips. Add to the mango. Coarsely chop the fresh coriander or mint and stir into the mango and onion. Cut 1 jalapeño pepper in half and finely chop; slice the other jalapeños into thin rings. Add the chopped jalapeños to the salsa. Cut 1 lime into 8 wedges. Grate the zest of the other lime into the mango salsa, then cut the lime in half and squeeze in the juice. Stir in the ginger syrup and sunflower oil. Taste, and season with pepper and salt. Let the salsa stand so the flavours can develop (at least 15 minutes but preferably 2 hours).

Preheat the oven to 120 °C. Cut each of the Raw Burgers into 4 pieces and shape them into balls, then flatten the balls into patties. Press 3 to 4 jalapeño rings into each patty.

Heat a splash of sunflower oil in 1 or 2 large frying pans and fry the patties (in 2 or 3 batches) for 3 to 4 minutes, turning, until browned on both sides. Keep them warm in the oven while you're frying the rest.

Arrange the patties on a platter with the jalapeño-side up, and spoon a little salsa onto each one.

Tip: You can also add chopped fresh coriander and/or dill to the vegan Burger meat.

Steak a claim to these sublimely spicy vegan patties made from Raw Burgers. If you want to turn down the heat, you can cut back on the jalapeños.

2 servings 20 minutes

CRISPY PANKO-FRIED VEGAN CHICKEN CHUNKS WITH WASABI MAYONNAISE

200 g rice flour
3 tbsp paprika (powder)
freshly ground black pepper and salt
150–200 g panko (Japanese breadcrumbs)
1 pack (160 g) vegan Chicken Chunks by The Vegetarian Butcher
8 tbsp vegan mayonnaise
2 tbsp soy sauce
1–2 tbsp wasabi
oil for deep-frying

Also needed: deep fryer or other pan for deep-frying; kitchen thermometer

Put 75 grams rice flour into a deep plate. Very gradually stir in 140 millilitres of cold water so that you have a thin paste with no lumps. Stir in the paprika, a generous amount of pepper, and a pinch of salt.

Sprinkle the panko into a deep plate, and the remaining rice flour onto a saucer. Coat the Chicken Chunks by first dipping them lightly in the rice flour, then in the paste, and finally, in the panko. Place them side by side on a plate or tray.

In a bowl, mix the mayonnaise with the soy sauce and wasabi to taste. The more wasabi you use, the hotter it will be.

Heat the oil to around 170 °C. (Use a kitchen thermometer if you're deep-frying in an ordinary pan.) Deep-fry the Chicken Chunks (about 6 at a time) for 3 to 4 minutes until very light brown. Allow them to drain on kitchen paper. Serve with the wasabi mayonnaise.

Tip: You can also sprinkle the crunchy Chicken Chunks with a little finely chopped chives or chervil.

Everybody loves deep-fried chicken, and it's especially popular in Japan. Panko – light, flaky breadcrumbs – is used in Japanese cooking to give food a pleasant crunch. But you'd better shake a leg, because these snacks will be gone in a flash!

4 servings (main dish) 50 minutes

VEGAN SCOTTISH BRIDIES WITH PICCALILLI

1 onion
25 g vegan margarine
6 vegan Raw Burgers by The Vegetarian Butcher
freshly ground black pepper and salt
2–4 tsp mustard powder
1 tbsp steak seasoning
2 rolls (about 230 g each) savoury shortcrust pastry sheets (refrigerator section)
piccalilli

Peel and finely chop the onion. Heat the margarine in a frying pan over fairly high heat and fry the onion for 3 to 4 minutes until slightly browned.

Put the Raw Burgers into a large bowl and add a generous amount of pepper, 1 teaspoon salt, 2 to 4 teaspoons mustard powder (to taste), the steak seasoning, and the fried onion. Mix well, then divide the mince mixture into 4 pieces.

Place the sheets of pastry on the worktop, and cut them in half lengthwise. Leave them on the baking paper. Cut out the largest possible oval from each piece of pastry. Distribute the mince mixture over one half of each of the 4 ovals, staying back 1 ½ cm from the edges. Moisten the edges of the pastry around the filling with a tiny bit of cold water, then fold the other half of the pastry ovals over the filling. With a fork, press down firmly on the edges. Put the bridies in the fridge until use.

Preheat the oven to 180 °C forty-five minutes before you would like to serve the bridies. Bake them for 25 to 30 minutes until golden brown and cooked through.

Put them onto plates and serve along with the piccalilli.

Tip: Bridies are wonderful made in the traditional way, but are also delicious if you vary the seasoning. Try using herbes de Provence, ras el hanout, curry powder, or Cajun or Mexican seasoning.

These traditional Scottish meat pies can be eaten either hot or cold. Eaten cold, they're handy for taking on trips or to school or work for lunch, and are a natural for picnics.

12–14 pieces (snack or appetizer) 30 minutes + cooling time

VEGAN CRISPY CHICKEN BURGER TAMAKI SUSHI WITH WASABI MAYO

250 g sushi rice
20 g agave syrup
freshly ground black pepper and salt
3 tbsp vegan mayonnaise
¾–1 ½ tsp wasabi (Asian supermarket)
6–8 nori sheets (seaweed; Asian supermarket)
splash of corn oil
6 vegan Crispy Chicken Burgers by The Vegetarian Butcher
12 smallish curly endive (frisée) leaves
3 tbsp ready-made seaweed salad (Asian supermarket)
2 tbsp thin strips of carrot
Japanese soy sauce

Wash the rice several times until the water runs clear, then let the rice soak for 1 hour. In a narrow high-sided pan, bring 375 millilitres of cold water to a boil along with the washed rice and a pinch of salt. Stir, then place a clean ironed tea towel over the top of the pan and cover with the lid. Fold the corners of the tea towel up and over the lid so that they don't touch the stovetop's heat source. Allow the rice to cook, covered, over very low heat for about 15 to 20 minutes until done. Remove the pan remove from the heat and allow to stand for another 10 minutes, covered.

Spoon the rice onto a platter. In a bowl, mix the white wine vinegar and agave syrup with a little salt and pepper. Gently stir this into the rice. Then stir the rice every 5 minutes until it has reached room temperature.

Meanwhile, mix the mayonnaise with wasabi to taste (the more you add, the hotter it will be). Cut the sheets of nori in half with a scissors so that you end up with long rectangles. Place the sheets side by side on the worktop, shiny side down, with the long edge towards you.
Heat a splash of corn oil in a large frying pan over medium heat and fry the Crispy Chicken Burgers for about 6 minutes, turning, until crisp and golden brown on both sides. Transfer them to a cutting board and cut each one into 6 to 8 strips.

Have a bowl of water ready so you can clean your fingers from time to time. Spread the rice with your fingers into a thin, even layer (½-cm thick) over three-quarters of the surface of the nori sheets, leaving the right-hand side uncovered.

Place the lettuce leaves on the left-hand side of the rice so that they extend slightly over the top edge. Spoon on a thin diagonal line of wasabi mayo, going from the bottom to the top. Then add the seaweed salad, carrot strips, and 2 to 3 strips of Crispy Chicken Burger, which can also extend over the top edge. Starting from the left, fold over one corner of the filled nori sheet, then roll up fairly tightly into a cone.

Serve at once, along with the soy sauce and the rest of the wasabi mayo as a dip for the rolls.

Tip: Delicious served with pickled ginger.

10 servings (snack or lunch dish) 50 minutes

CURRIED VEGAN SAUSAGE ROLLS

6 sprigs of fresh coriander (cilantro) or flat-leaf parsley
4 vegan Raw Burgers by The Vegetarian Butcher
2 tbsp mild curry powder
6 tbsp mango chutney
freshly ground black pepper and salt
10 vegan puff pastry squares (about 12½ x 12½ cm; freezer section, thawed)

Also needed: baking paper; clean scissors

Roughly chop the herbs. Place the Raw Burgers in a large bowl. Add the chopped herbs, curry powder, and the mango chutney and mix well. Before assembling the sausage rolls, you can taste the mixture first by frying a heaping tablespoon of the mixture in a frying pan over medium heat for 2 minutes on both sides. Taste, and if necessary season the rest of the mixture with a little more pepper and salt.

On the worktop, place the puff pastry squares side by side on a sheet of baking paper. Shape the mince mixture into 10 rolls, 11 cm long. Place these rolls in the middle of the puff pastry squares. Moisten the puff pastry lightly on one side of the rolls with a tiny bit of cold water. Fold the dry side of the pastry over the rolls so that the edges line up evenly, then press down firmly on these edges with a fork. With a scissors, snip a row of 5 small v's down the centre of each sausage roll. Place the sausage rolls (on the baking paper) on a baking tray in the fridge until use.

Preheat the oven to 180 °C forty-five minutes before you would like to serve the sausage rolls. Bake for 25 to 30 minutes until golden brown and cooked through.

Tip: Make mini sausage rolls by cutting the puff pastry squares into 4 pieces and making 40 small sausage rolls.

We'd like to take a bow – not a cow! – for this recipe. Let's give this vegan sausage roll seasoned with curry a big round of applause. For variations on this twist, try using other spice mixtures such as ras el hanout, herbes de Provence, garam masala (Indian spice powder blend), or Mexican or Cajun seasoning.

'It makes me happy when I can make other people happy with my food.'

Roepa Sonai is an old hand at The Vegetarian Butcher, and has wielded her cleaver there for years. With her extensive practical experience, Roepa is one of the foremost authorities when it comes to working with the new plant-based meat.

I was working in a bank when my daughter-in-law told me about a job opening at The Vegetarian Butcher. She always ordered their products online. I'm a long-time vegetarian, and I immediately thought this might be something for me. I went straight over – they had a new warehouse and it wasn't even really finished yet, but when I stepped inside I knew at once: I want to work here.

To start with, my job was to test what happened to our products over time: what if the vegan Chicken Chunks had been frozen for a while? Because I love to cook, I became the one who made lunch every Wednesday for all of our staff and guests. In the beginning there were around sixty-five people, but that number kept going up. *Give it to Roepa*, they might say when there is a new product to test. Just give me good ingredients, and I'll always make it into something delicious. This is something I've learned during my time at The Vegetarian Butcher: it makes me happy when I can make other people happy with my food. To see the joy on their faces.

They call me the unifying force within the company, and that makes me very proud. I'm sixty-five now and so I'm gradually moving towards retirement, but I'd much rather keep working for a few more years.

My vegetarian curried chicken is everybody's favourite, so that's what I'm going to make for this cookbook. And I would like to dedicate this recipe to my grandchildren, who are almost completely vegetarian by now. I made this curried chicken often during my early days at The Vegetarian Butcher. Meetings would even be planned for a Wednesday so that guests could join us for lunch. If everyone starts eating like that, the future looks bright!

ROEPA COOKS: **CURRIED VEGAN CHICKEN CHUNK ROLLS**

4 servings (main dish) 40 minutes

CURRIED VEGAN CHICKEN CHUNK ROLLS

1 large onion
3 garlic cloves
3 sprigs of celery leaves
sunflower oil
1 heaped tbsp curry masala powder
(Surinamese or other curry powder)
2 vegetable stock cubes
1 Madame Jeanette (very hot pepper!)
1 level tsp freshly ground black pepper
1 level tsp (freshly) ground white pepper
2 packs (160 g each) vegan Chicken Chunks
by The Vegetarian Butcher
4 vegan slightly crusty oval white bread rolls
mixed pickles
yellow hot thick pepper sauce
(such as Madame Jeanette sambal)

Peel the onion and garlic. Finely chop the onion. Squeeze the garlic through a garlic press. Finely chop the celery leaves.

In a heavy-bottomed pan, heat a generous splash of sunflower oil over medium heat. Add the onions and garlic to the pan, and fry for 3 to 4 minutes until the onion is translucent and starts to brown. Stir in the curry masala powder, and immediately add a cup of hot water to keep the curry powder from burning.

Crumble the stock cubes into the pan. Add the celery leaves, the whole Madame Jeanette, and the black and white pepper. Then pour in 400 millilitres of hot water. Bring nearly to a boil, and allow to simmer for 20 minutes over fairly low heat.

Add the Chicken Chunks and continue simmering for another 10 minutes over low heat until they are tender and around three-quarters of the liquid has evaporated.

Remove Madame Jeanette pepper. Slice open the bread rolls, and fill them with the curried Chicken Chunks. Garnish with a bit of pickle and a dab of hot pepper sauce, or top with a piece of the Madame Jeanette pepper.

6 empanadas | 1 hour

VEGAN CHICKEN CHUNK EMPANADAS

1 onion
2 garlic cloves
1 pack (160 g) vegan Chicken Chunks by The Vegetarian Butcher
1 small tin (about 200 g) corn kernels
sunflower oil
1 ½ tsp chilli powder
1 tbsp smoked paprika (powder)
1 tbsp tomato paste
3 sprigs of fresh oregano or 1 ½ tsp dried oregano
10 sprigs of flat-leaf parsley
300 g vegan savoury shortcrust pastry (pie crust dough; ready-made or homemade*)

* To make the shortcrust pastry yourself: In a bowl, mix together 250 g flour, 75 g vegan margarine, 50 ml almond milk, 50 ml water, and a pinch of salt. Knead together briefly until the dough comes together.

Preheat the oven to 180 °C.

Peel and finely chop the onion and garlic. Cut the Chicken Chunks into slightly smaller pieces. Drain the corn. Heat a splash of sunflower oil in a large frying pan. Fry the onion over medium heat for 3 minutes until translucent. Stir in the garlic, Chicken Chunks, corn, the chilli and paprika. Fry for 3 minutes more. Stir in the tomato paste and fry for another 2 minutes. Add the oregano and ½ cup water and allow to cook gently for 4 to 5 minutes until the liquid has evaporated and the mixture is no longer wet.

Coarsely chop the parsley and stir into the Chicken Chunk filling. Taste, and season with pepper and salt if desired.

Divide the pastry dough into 6 pieces, and roll them out into thin circles (about 15 cm Ø). Spoon one sixth of the filling in to the middle of each dough circle, staying back 3 to 4 cm from the edges. Moisten the edges with a little cold water. Fold the dough over the filling, and press the edges firmly with a fork to seal. Place them on a baking sheet lined with baking paper. Bake for 20 to 25 minutes until light brown.

You'll fall hard for these delicious empanadas filled with juicy vegan Chicken Chunks and corn. Because you can eat them with your hands, empanadas are the ultimate take-along snack.

36–40 dumplings 1 hour and 15 minutes

VEGAN CHICKEN CHUNK GYOZAS

2 packs (160 g each) vegan Chicken Chunks by The Vegetarian Butcher
3 spring onions
300 g pointed cabbage (from the pointed end of the cabbage)
2 garlic cloves
a piece (about 40 g) of fresh ginger
2 tbsp rice flour or cornflour
7 tbsp salty soy sauce
2½ tbsp sesame oil
4 tbsp mirin (Japanese cooking wine) or sake
1 package (about 300 g) round gyoza or wonton wrappers (freezer section; Asian supermarket, thawed)
1–2 tbsp rice or white wine vinegar
sunflower oil

Also needed: food processor or hand blender with blending cup; clean straining cloth or tea towel (ironed with a hot iron)

Mince the Chicken Chunks. Clean the spring onions and cut into pieces. Slice a few of the green pieces into thin rings for the dipping sauce, and set aside. Cut the pointed cabbage into pieces as well. Peel and finely chop the garlic. Peel and coarsely chop the ginger. In a food processor or blending jar of a hand blender, process the pieces of spring onion, pointed cabbage, garlic, and ginger until very fine. Put the mixture into the centre of the straining cloth or tea towel. Gather together the corners and lift over the sink, turning and squeezing to remove as much liquid as possible. Then put this cabbage mixture into a bowl and mix with the Chicken Chunks, the rice flour or cornflour, 1 tablespoon soy sauce, 1½ tablespoons sesame oil, and 2 tablespoons mirin or sake.

Place 1 gyoza or wonton wrapper on the palm of your hand and put 1½ teaspoons filling in the middle of the wrapper. Moisten the edges with a tiny bit of cold water, fold the wrapper over the filling, press the edges together to seal, and fold pleats into the edges. Repeat for the rest of the gyozas, using all of the filling, and put them on a plate covered with baking paper (side by side, leaving some space in between). Cover and refrigerate until needed.

For the dipping sauce, mix the remaining soy sauce with the rest of the sesame oil, 1 to 2 tablespoon(s) vinegar, and the spring onion rings.

Heat a splash of sunflower oil in a large frying pan and fry batches of gyozas over high heat until they are flecked with brown spots all over. Then add 4 to 6 tablespoons warm water to the pan between (not over) the gyozas and cover with a lid. Heat for 3 to 4 minutes. Remove the lid and wait until the liquid has evaporated and the gyozas are done. If necessary, add another 1 to 2 tablespoons water. Serve with the dipping sauce.

10–20 servings   35 minutes

VEGETARIAN MEATBALL SATAY WITH THAI PEANUT DIP

1 juicy organic lime
a piece (about 30 g) of fresh ginger
1 garlic clove
1 ½ tbsp ginger syrup
1–3 tsp hot thick pepper sauce (such as sambal oelek)
2 tbsp salty soy sauce
groundnut (peanut) or sunflower oil
150 g peanuts
2 packs (170 g each) vegetarian Meatballs by The Vegetarian Butcher
12 sprigs of chives

Also needed: barbecue, grill, griddle, or grill pan; 8 skewers (soaked in water for 30 minutes)

Light the barbecue or preheat the grill to the highest setting. (You can also use a griddle or grill pan.)

Start with the soy sauce marinade. Grate the zest of the lime, then cut the lime in half and juice both halves. Peel and grate the ginger. Peel the garlic and squeeze through a garlic press into a large dish. Mix in half of the grated lime zest, 2 teaspoons grated ginger, 1 tablespoon lime juice, 1 ½ teaspoons ginger syrup, hot pepper sauce to taste, 1 ½ tablespoons soy sauce, and 3 tablespoons oil.

For the Thai peanut dip, coarsely chop the peanuts and mix with the remaining lime juice and zest and the remaining soy sauce and ginger syrup. Add pepper sauce to taste along with 2 to 3 tablespoons cold water. Stir well.

Cut the Meatballs into 4 pieces and thread them onto the skewers. Brush the Meatball skewers (with the pastry brush) with the soy sauce marinade on all sides. Allow to stand for 2 to 3 minutes. Then brush them again with the marinade and let them stand for another 2 to 3 minutes. Brush them again, and grill for 3 to 4 minutes until browned on all sides. Turn them regularly, and continue to brush or drizzle with the soy sauce marinade.

Place the Meatball satay on a platter, snip lengths of chives over the skewers, and serve with the peanut sauce.

Tip: Delicious served with cassava crackers, cucumber-carrot salad, and rice or noodles. Give the peanut dip your own twist. You can keep it on the dry side, or make it creamier by stirring in a dash of stock.

These vegetarian Meatball satay skewers are grilled on the barbecue or under the grill, and brushed repeatedly with flavourful soy sauce marinade. Now that's excellent ball control.

6 servings (snack or appetizer) 40 minutes

VEGAN CHICKEN AND RED ONION BHAJIS

2 vegan Chicken Breasts by The Vegetarian Butcher
½-1 tsp chilli powder
pinch of ground turmeric
1 tsp ground cumin
1 small green chilli pepper
3 medium red onions
freshly ground black pepper and salt
100 g white flour
1 ½ tsp baking powder
vegetable oil for deep-frying

Also needed: deep fryer or other pan for deep-frying; kitchen thermometer

Cut the Chicken Breasts into matchsticks. Mix them with the chilli powder, ground turmeric, and ground cumin and set them aside.

Meanwhile, finely chop the green chilli pepper (stem, seeds, and membranes removed). Peel the onions and slice them into very thin rings. Place them on a clean tea towel and sprinkle them with a little salt. Wrap the tea towel tightly around the onions, crushing them slightly. Then mix them with the chilli pepper and Chicken Breast matchsticks.

Sift the flour and baking powder into a bowl. Stir in 100 millilitres of cold water by first adding three-quarters of the water, then very gradually adding in the rest. The batter should be thick but not too stiff, so that it coats the other ingredients well. This may require adding a bit less or a bit more water.

Shortly before you plan to eat the bhajis, heat the oil in the deep fryer or other pan to about 170 °C. Stir the Chicken Breast-onion mixture into the batter. Carefully lower heaped tablespoons of the mixture into the oil, using another tablespoon to push the mixture off the spoon. Fry 5 or 6 bhajis at a time for about 4 to 5 minutes until brown all over and cooked through.

Delicious served with raita (recipe on page 200) or fresh coriander and yoghurt sauce: Mix 150 millilitres of vegan yoghurt with 5 tablespoons coarsely chopped fresh coriander (cilantro), 1 tablespoon chopped mint, 1 tablespoon lime juice, 1 tablespoon ginger syrup (Asian supermarket, or use syrup from a jar of preserved ginger), a generous pinch of salt, and a bit of chilli powder.

Thank god it's Fry-day! These vegan chicken and onion fritters are deep-fried until they're slightly crisp on the outside, but still somewhat soft on the inside. That's when they're at their best. You can eat them as they are, or dip them in a zippy vegan sauce.

about 24 pieces (snack or appetizer) 45 minutes

VEGAN CHICKEN SAMOSAS WITH MINT AND RAITA

1 medium floury potato
3 medium carrots
2 vegan Chicken Breasts by The Vegetarian Butcher
small bunch of mint
freshly ground black pepper and salt
groundnut (peanut) oil
1 tbsp Madras curry powder (mild or hot)
100 g peas (cooked fresh peas or frozen)
24 samosa wrappers or 8 large spring roll wrappers (about 25 cm)
2 garlic cloves
1 cucumber
1 small lemon
150 g vegan yoghurt

Also needed: pastry brush; grater

Peel the potato and carrots and cut them into small cubes of around 1 cm. Then cut the Chicken Breasts into 1-cm pieces as well. Remove the leaves from the sprigs of mint and finely chop.

Heat a splash of groundnut oil in a large frying pan over high heat and stir-fry the pieces of Chicken Breast with the curry powder and a pinch of salt for 3 minutes. Add the cubes of potato and carrot. Pour in just enough hot water to cover, cover the pan with a lid, and cook for about 10 minutes until the potato cubes are tender. Remove the lid and continue to cook a little longer over high heat until all of the liquid has evaporated. Taste, and season with pepper and salt. Stir in the peas and 2 tablespoons chopped mint.

Place the wrappers side by side on the worktop with the narrow side towards you (if you're using spring roll wrappers, first cut them into 3 equal strips). Put a spoonful of the curried Chicken Breast mixture at the bottom of each wrapper. Using the pastry brush, moisten the rest of the wrapper with a tiny bit of cold water. Fold the part of the wrapper with the filling diagonally to form a triangle, then keep folding tightly so that you end up with compact triangular parcels. Moisten the last part of the wrapper with a tiny bit of water and seal.

Make the raita: Peel the garlic and squeeze it through the garlic press into a small bowl. Heat a small splash of oil in a small frying pan over medium heat and fry two-thirds of the garlic for about 1 minute until light brown (set aside the rest of the garlic). Peel the cucumber and grate it into a colander. Sprinkle the cucumber with a bit of salt and allow to drain well for 10 minutes. Wash the lemon and grate the zest into the bowl with the garlic you've set aside. Cut the lemon in half, and squeeze 1 of the halves into the bowl. Stir in the drained grated cucumber, the rest of the mint, the fried garlic, and the vegan yoghurt. Taste, and season with pepper, salt, and a little more lemon juice if desired.

Shortly before you want to serve the samosas, heat a generous layer of oil in a large high-sided frying pan over medium heat and fry them for a few minutes, turning, until crisp and golden brown.

Serve with the raita.

6 servings (snack) 30 minutes

LOUISIANA VEGAN MEAT BITES WITH CORN

4 spring onions
1 red (bell) pepper
6 sprigs of fresh coriander (cilantro) or flat-leaf parsley
1 tin (140 g) corn kernels
4 vegan Raw Burgers by The Vegetarian Butcher
3½ tbsp Cajun seasoning
8 tbsp tomato ketchup
freshly ground black pepper and salt
200 g rice flour
100–150 g coarse dried breadcrumbs
oil for deep-frying

Also needed: deep fryer or other pan; kitchen thermometer

Very finely chop the spring onion and red pepper, and coarsely chop the herbs. Allow the corn to drain well.

Put the Raw Burgers into a large bowl, and add 2 tablespoons Cajun seasoning, 1 teaspoon salt, three-quarters of the spring onion, a quarter of the pepper, half of the chopped herbs, and the corn. Mix until thoroughly combined. Shape the mince mixture into 18 small sausages around 1½ cm thick. Put them in the fridge for now. Mix the tomato ketchup with the remaining spring onion, pepper, chopped herbs, and 1½ teaspoons Cajun seasoning. Taste, and season with pepper and salt if desired.

Put 75 grams rice flour into a deep plate. Very gradually stir in 200 millilitres of cold water so that you have a thin paste with no lumps. Stir in the final tablespoon of Cajun seasoning and a pinch of salt.

Sprinkle the dried breadcrumbs into a deep plate, and the remaining rice flour onto a saucer. Coat the 'sausages' by first dipping them lightly in the saucer of rice flour, then in the rice flour paste, and finally in the dried breadcrumbs. Place them side by side on a plate or tray.

Heat the oil in the deep fryer or pan to about 170 °C shortly before you'd like to serve the bites. Deep-fry them (no more than 6 at a time) in the hot oil for 3 to 4 minutes until they're light brown. Allow to drain on kitchen paper.

Serve along with the sauce.

Let's get to the meat of the matter – these Louisiana vegan meat bites are crispy, juicy, and spicy. Delightful, delectable mouthfuls of flavour, they can be served as a snack, as tapas, or as an appetizer.

CLASSICS

VEGAN WELLINGTON WITH MUSHROOMS

6–8 servings (main dish) 2 hours

---

2 medium onions
3 garlic cloves
2 sprigs of rosemary
700 g chestnut mushrooms (cremini)
75 g blanched hazelnuts
2 tbsp rapeseed (canola) or sunflower oil
2 organic oranges
1 tin (400 g) chickpeas, with liquid
1 vegetable stock cube
8 sprigs of tarragon
8 sprigs of flat-leaf parsley
freshly ground black pepper and salt
8 vegan Raw Burgers by The Vegetarian Butcher
3½ tsp mustard
2 tbsp agave syrup
2 large rolls (350 g each) vegan puff pastry

Also needed: hand blender with blending cup or liquidizer (blender)

Peel and finely chop the onions and garlic. Remove the needles from the rosemary sprigs and coarsely chop. Finely chop the mushrooms. Coarsely chop the hazelnuts. Heat a splash of oil in a large frying pan. Add the onion, garlic, hazelnuts, and rosemary and fry over high heat for 3 minutes until they just start to brown. Grate the zest of the oranges into the pan and fry over low heat for 2 minutes more. Juice the oranges. Drain the liquid from the chickpeas into a measuring jug.

Spoon half of the onion-rosemary mixture into a large dish. Add the mushrooms and another splash of oil to the frying pan, and stir-fry for about 4 minutes until slightly browned. Crumble the stock cube into the mushrooms, and add 75 millilitres of the chickpea liquid and the orange juice to the pan. Stir together and cook for 4 to 5 minutes until most of the liquid has evaporated and about 3 tablespoons of the liquid remains. Finely chop the tarragon and parsley. With the hand blender or liquidizer, puree the chickpeas and about 5 tablespoons of the chickpea liquid into a thick puree (if it's too thick to blend, add more chickpea liquid). Stir the puree into the mushroom mixture, then stir in the tarragon and parsley. Taste, and season with salt and pepper.

Put the Raw Burgers into the dish with the onion-rosemary mixture. Add 1½ teaspoons mustard. Mix well, and shape into a roll 25 cm long. Flatten the roll slightly.

Unroll the dough from one package of puff pastry and place it on a baking sheet lined with baking paper. Spoon a third of the mushroom mixture onto the middle of the puff pastry to form a long, wide row (about 25 x 15 cm). Place the Burger roll on top. Cover the top and sides of the roll with the rest of the mushroom mixture. With a very small amount of cold water, moisten the edges of the puff pastry around the filling. Unroll the dough from the other package of puff pastry and place it on top, fitting it gently but firmly over the filling. Seal the edges of the 2 layers by pressing down with a fork. Then trim around the edges to form an oval. Make 3 small holes at the top to allow any steam to escape. To decorate, you can score the pastry here and there with the back of a knife (not too deep – it shouldn't cut through the dough). Refrigerate the vegan Wellington for at least 30 minutes.

Preheat the oven to 200 °C. Mix the remaining mustard with the agave syrup and brush onto the pastry. Bake for about 45 minutes until golden brown and cooked through. Remove from the oven and allow to rest for 5 to 10 minutes. Cut into thick slices and serve.

4 servings (main dish) 1 hour and 10 minutes

VEGAN CHICKEN PROVENÇAL WITH ARTICHOKES AND OLIVES

6 small red onions
3 garlic cloves
3 large overripe tomatoes
1 tin (about 400 g) artichoke hearts
50 g vegan margarine
4 vegan Chicken Breasts
by The Vegetarian Butcher
4 tbsp sun-dried tomatoes in oil
250 g stoned mixed olives
3 tbsp dried herbes de Provence or
a small bunch of fresh herbs
250 ml full-bodied red wine
1 vegetable stock cube
freshly ground black pepper

Also needed: casserole (Dutch oven)

Peel the onions and cut each onion into 6 wedges. Peel and finely chop the garlic. Cut the tomatoes into small cubes, saving the juice. Cut the artichoke hearts into 6 wedges.

Heat the margarine in the casserole over medium heat. When the margarine turns brown, fry the Chicken Breasts for a few minutes, turning, until brown on both sides.

Add the wedges of onion and the finely chopped garlic to the pan with the Chicken Breasts and fry 3 minutes more. Stir frequently. Then add the fresh tomato pieces, saved tomato juice, the sun-dried tomato, the olives, and the herbes de Provence. (If you're using fresh herbs, you can add the sprigs to the pan whole, after rinsing them first.)

Pour the wine and 150 millilitres of cold water into the pan, crumble in the stock cube, and sprinkle in plenty of pepper. Stir together, bring just to a boil, and allow to gently simmer over very low heat for 45 minutes. After 35 minutes, add the artichoke hearts.

Wonderful served with rice, pasta, potatoes, or crusty brown bread.

Chicken and herbes de Provence are a match made in heaven. Although herbes de Provence are usually bought as a ready-made blend, it's more fun and also tastier to make your own using fresh or dried herbs. You can use the following proportions as a guide: 2 parts marjoram; 2 parts thyme; 2 parts savory; 1 part rosemary; 1 part basil; and slightly less sage and (if you have them on hand) lavender flowers.

8 servings (main dish) 2 hours and 15 minutes

VEGAN BURGER BOURGUIGNON

3 large carrots
4 medium red onions
4 garlic cloves
400 g white mushrooms
12 vegan Raw Burgers by The Vegetarian Butcher
75 g vegan margarine
1 jar (340 g) large sweet pickled silverskin (pearl) onions
1 tin (70 g) tomato paste
12 sprigs of thyme
3 bay leaves
4 tbsp dried porcini mushrooms (boletus)
freshly ground black pepper and salt
750 ml full-bodied, fruity red wine

Also needed: large casserole (Dutch oven)

Peel the carrots and cut them into 1½- to 2-cm slices. Peel the onions and slice them into thin rings. Peel and finely chop the garlic. Clean the white mushrooms. Cut large ones in half and leave small ones whole. Cut each Raw Burger into 6 pieces. Drain the liquid from the pickled onions into a small jug.

Melt the margarine in a casserole. Once the margarine has browned and any foaming has reduced, fry the Burger pieces for about 4 minutes until browned on all sides. Remove from the pan. Add the carrot and onion to the pan, and stir-fry them for 5 minutes. Add the garlic and white mushrooms and fry for 3 minutes more. Stir in the pickled onions.

Stir in the tomato paste and continue stirring as you fry for 1 minute more. Remove the leaves from the thyme sprigs over the pan (or tie the sprigs together with butcher's twine and add them to the pan). Add the bay leaves and dried porcini mushrooms (don't soak them in advance!). Sprinkle in ½ teaspoon pepper and ½ teaspoon salt. Pour in the wine and bring to a boil. Stir in the fried Burger pieces and allow to simmer over very low heat for 2 hours. Taste, and season with some of the liquid from the pickled onions and a little pepper and salt. If using whole thyme sprigs, remove them before serving.

Tip: Delicious served with creamy mashed potatoes, floury boiled potatoes, gnocchi, or pasta. This Burger stew tastes even better if you make it a day or two in advance.

At The Vegetarian Butcher, we left the cow out of the bourguignon, but kept the crowds at the table when it's served. This dish is ideal if you're cooking for a group – you're sure to delight your guests. It truly has a wow factor (without a cow factor!).

6–8 servings (main dish) 1 hour and 15 minutes

VEGAN SUNDAY MEATLOAF WITH MUSHROOM GRAVY

1 bunch (about 30 g) mixed fresh Italian herbs
3 garlic cloves
10 vegan Raw Burgers by The Vegetarian Butcher
2 tbsp mustard
about 65 g vegan margarine (cold from the fridge)
500 ml vegetable stock
1 onion
300 g mixed mushrooms
30 g dried porcini mushrooms (boletus)
freshly ground black pepper and salt

Also needed: small fireproof roasting tin

Preheat the oven to 170 °C. Remove the leaves from the sprigs of herbs and finely chop. Peel and finely chop the garlic.

Put the Raw Burgers into a large bowl along with the herbs, half of the garlic, and 1 tablespoon mustard and knead everything together. Shape this meatloaf mixture into an oval loaf of around 7 (high) x 11 (wide) x 20 (long) cm. Place a few chunks of margarine in the roasting tin; put the meatloaf on top of these chunks, and place a few chunks of margarine on top of the meatloaf (around 40 grams margarine in total). Then add a generous splash of the stock. Put the meatloaf in the oven and bake for 55 to 65 minutes until done. Spoon over some of the juices from the roasting tin at regular intervals. Add a little more stock if the roasting tin gets too dry while the meatloaf is baking. Meanwhile, peel and finely chop the onion. Clean the fresh mushrooms and cut them into large chunks.

Heat a chunk of margarine in a frying pan and stir-fry the onion with the remaining garlic for 3 minutes over medium heat until translucent. Increase the heat to high. Add the fresh mushrooms and stir-fry for 2 minutes more. Add 300 millilitres of stock and the dried mushrooms (don't soak them in advance!). Bring nearly to a boil and allow to cook gently for 5 minutes. Turn off the heat and allow to stand until the meatloaf is done.

Take the meatloaf out of the roasting tin and place it on a cutting board. Place the roasting tin over high heat. Add the stock with mushrooms to the pan juices in the roasting tin and bring to a boil while stirring. Stir in the remaining mustard to taste, then stir in another 25 grams margarine (divided into 4 chunks), one chunk at a time. Allow to come briefly to a boil. Taste, and season with pepper and salt.

Cut the meatloaf into thick slices and serve with the mushroom gravy.

Tip: Good served with potatoes cooked in their jackets and green beans, peas, or a salad.

'Meatloaf' sounds like 'meat love', and that's exactly what we're showing here: our love for meat, the plant-based way.

6 servings (main dish) 1 hour and 20 minutes

VEGAN CHICKEN CHUNK COQ AU VIN

1 onion
1 garlic clove
100 g (about 3) small carrots
50 g smoked almonds
70 g vegan margarine
freshly ground black pepper and salt
2 bay leaves
6 sprigs of thyme
1 tbsp dried herbes de Provence
300 ml dry white wine or red wine
300 ml vegan cooking cream
30 g dried mixed mushrooms
3 packs (160 g each) vegan Chicken Chunks by The Vegetarian Butcher

Peel and finely chop the onion and garlic. Cut the carrots into slices. Coarsely chop the almonds.

Melt 30 grams margarine in a deep casserole. When the margarine has browned, stir-fry the onion and carrot with a little pepper and a pinch of salt over fairly high heat for 3 to 4 minutes until they start to brown.

Stir in the almonds, bay leaves, thyme sprigs, garlic, and dried herbs. Increase the heat to high. Pour in the wine and allow to bubble briefly. Then pour in the cooking cream and stir in the dried mushrooms (don't soak them in advance!).

Bring to a boil, turn the heat down very low, and allow to simmer gently for 40 minutes. Stir occasionally. If the sauce starts to get too thick, add a small amount of water.

After 35 minutes, melt 40 grams margarine in a large frying pan and quickly stir-fry the Chicken Chunks over fairly high heat until browned. Add them to the pan with the other ingredients, stir, and simmer for 8 to 10 minutes more. Taste, and season with pepper and salt. Remove the bay leaves and thyme.

Tip: Wonderful served with pasta, rice, or mashed or boiled potatoes.

If you ask us, the bird-based version in red or white wine is nothing to crow about. But we'd do the funky chicken for our vegan coq au vin! We live (and let live) for classics like this.

CLASSICS

6–8 servings (main dish) 30–60 minutes

SWEET AND SAVOURY BASTILLA WITH VEGAN CHICKEN CHUNKS AND ALMONDS

3 packs (160 g each) vegan Chicken Chunks by The Vegetarian Butcher
3 onions
1 bunch (about 15 g) flat-leaf parsley
sunflower oil
3 tbsp ras el hanout
1 organic lemon
150 g vegan margarine
500 g blanched almonds
1 ½ tsp cinnamon, plus extra
3 tbsp icing sugar (powdered sugar), plus extra
1 ½ tbsp orange flower water
freshly ground black pepper and salt
300 g silken tofu (Asian supermarket)
about 10 sheets (1 package, 250 g) of filo dough (freezer section, thawed)

Also needed: casserole (Dutch oven); food processor; bastilla tin or baking tin with raised rim (such as a tart tin), about 25–30 cm Ø

Cut the Chicken Chunks into strips. Peel the onions and grate or chop them until very fine. Finely chop the parsley. Heat a splash of sunflower oil in a casserole and fry the onion with the ras el hanout and parsley over very low heat for 5 minutes. Stir frequently. Add the Chicken Chunks, grate the lemon zest into the pan, and stir-fry everything for another 10 minutes.

Meanwhile, melt the margarine in a saucepan. Put 3 tablespoons of this melted margarine into a frying pan along with the almonds and fry them over medium heat until golden brown. Then process the almonds in a food processor until finely ground, and flavour with the cinnamon, icing sugar, and orange flower water.
Taste the Chicken Chunk mixture and season with pepper and salt. Coarsely mash the silken tofu and mix it in. Cut the lemon in half and squeeze in the juice of 1 of the halves.

Preheat the oven to 200 °C. Mix the remaining melted margarine with an equal amount of sunflower oil. Grease a large round bastilla tin or a baking tin with a raised rim with the margarine-oil. Brush both sides of 3 filo dough sheets with margarine-oil. Line the baking tin with these 3 sheets, placing them on top of each other crosswise so that the bottom and sides of the tin are completely covered. Allow the excess to hang over the edges of the tin. (You will fold this back over at the end to close up the bastilla.)

Distribute half of the almond mixture over the filo sheets. Brush 2 more filo sheets with the margarine-oil, then cover the mixture with these sheets, one on top of the other. Add the Chicken Chunk filling to the tin and distribute evenly, then cover as before with 2 filo sheets brushed with margarine-oil, fitting them over the filling. Spoon in the remaining almond mixture. Fold the overhanging pieces of filo over the filling. Brush 3 filo sheets with margarine-oil. Fold these sheets over and around the bastilla in the tin, wrapping it up as well as you can. Bake the bastilla in the middle of the hot oven for 20 minutes until crisp and golden brown. Transfer to a platter and sprinkle with icing sugar and cinnamon.

4-5 servings (main dish) 1 hour

VEGAN CHICKEN AND MIXED MUSHROOM PIE

150 ml white port
40 g dried mixed mushrooms
4 vegan Chicken Breasts by The Vegetarian Butcher
2 garlic cloves
1 leek
250 g fresh mixed mushrooms
50 g vegan margarine
1 ½ tbsp fresh or dried Italian herbs
250 ml vegan cooking cream
1 vegetable stock cube
3–4 tbsp cornstarch
1–2 tbsp coarse mustard
1 roll (about 250 g) vegan puff pastry, rolled out (refrigerator section)
freshly ground black pepper and salt

Also needed: ovenproof baking dish (1 ½–2 l capacity) or pie dish, preferably with a wide rim

Heat the white port in a small saucepan over low heat until lukewarm. Turn off the heat, add the dried mushrooms, and soak for 15 minutes.

Cut the Chicken Breasts into pieces of about 3 cm. Peel and finely chop the garlic. Slice the leek into thin rings. Clean the fresh mushrooms. Cut large mushrooms into chunks and leave small ones whole.

Melt the margarine in a large frying pan over medium heat. Wait until it browns, then stir-fry the Chicken Breast pieces for 2 to 3 minutes until golden brown. Add the garlic, fresh mushrooms, and the Italian herbs and stir-fry for 4 minutes. Stir in the leek, soaked mushrooms, and the liquid into the other ingredients in the pan. Allow to simmer for another 3 minutes.

Pour in the cooking cream, then crumble the stock cube into the pan. Stir, and bring just to a boil. Mix 2 to 3 tablespoons cornstarch with 2 to 3 tablespoons cold water to form a smooth paste, then add to the pan while stirring. Allow the ragout to simmer over low heat for another 5 minutes to thicken. Stir in 1 tablespoon mustard. Taste, and add more mustard and pepper and salt if desired. Turn off the heat and allow the ragout to cool for 15 minutes or longer. You can prepare the pie to this point in advance, and finish making it before you eat.

Preheat the oven to 200 °C. Spoon the cooled ragout into an ovenproof baking dish or pie dish. Cut a long strip, 1-cm wide, from one side of the puff pastry. Moisten the rim of the baking dish with a bit of cold water. Cover the rim with this puff pastry strip, and press down firmly. Then moisten the strip with a bit of cold water. Cover the dish with the puff pastry sheet, allowing it to hang over the edge of the dish, and trim off any of this excess pastry. Firmly press down on the rim of the dish with a fork to create a ribbed pattern. Make a hole in the centre of the pastry to allow the steam to escape (if you like, you can also put a tiny roll of baking paper into the hole to act as a chimney). Bake the pie for 30 to 35 minutes until golden brown.

4 servings (main dish) 20 minutes

SWISS GESCHNETZELTES WITH VEGAN CHICKEN CHUNKS AND CHANTERELLES

2 shallots
300 g chanterelles or white mushrooms
1 tbsp flour
1 tsp curry powder
2 packs (160 g each) vegan Chicken Chunks by The Vegetarian Butcher
50 g vegan margarine
freshly ground black pepper and salt
250 ml dry white wine
200 ml vegan cooking cream
2 sprigs of flat-leaf parsley

* How to make crispy homemade rösti: Peel and grate a few potatoes (waxy or floury, either will work). Put into a colander and mix with a little pepper and salt. Heat a thin layer of sunflower oil in a frying pan. Firmly squeeze the liquid out of about 3 tbsp of potato mixture at a time, place in small mounds in the hot sunflower oil, and flatten with the back of a spoon. Fry the röstis for a few minutes until golden brown on both sides and cooked through. Allow to drain on kitchen paper. Serve at once, or let the rösti cool and, when you're ready to serve them, reheat in a hot oven (200 °C) for 5 to 8 minutes.

Peel and finely chop the shallots. Clean the mushrooms. Cut only very large ones into chunks.

Mix the flour with the curry powder, and roll the Chicken Chunks in this mixture until lightly coated. Melt the margarine in a large frying pan over fairly high heat, and when it begins to brown, stir-fry the shallot, mushrooms, and Chicken Chunks for 5 minutes. Sprinkle with a little pepper. Increase the heat to high. Pour in the wine. Allow to bubble briefly, then pour in the cooking cream as you shake the pan back and forth. Allow to simmer gently for 2 to 3 minutes. Taste, and season with pepper and salt. If the sauce gets too thick, add a small amount of cold water, shaking the pan to mix well. Meanwhile, coarsely chop the parsley. Sprinkle over the Chicken Chunk geschnetzeltes.

Tip: While white mushrooms are often used (and that's just fine), it's even more delicious if you can manage to find chanterelles.

A little birdie told us that Switzerland is home to the world's first vegetarian restaurant. Hiltl was founded in 1898 in Zurich and is still going strong. In this quick Swiss classic dish, our vegan Chicken Chunks stay wonderfully juicy in the homemade white wine sauce. To make this meal truly complete, serve with homemade Swiss potato rösti*.

4 servings (main dish) 30 minutes

VEGAN BURGER SALTIMBOCCA

2 portobello mushrooms
1 garlic clove
1 tsp smoked paprika (powder)
freshly ground black pepper and salt
olive oil (also for deep-frying)
4 vegan Raw Burgers by The Vegetarian Butcher
3 sprigs of sage
100 g vegan margarine
150 ml dry white wine or sweet Marsala

Also needed: pastry brush; 8 cocktail sticks

Cut 2 thin round slices from the cap of each portobello. Cut the remainder of the caps and stems into chunks. Peel the garlic.

Mix the paprika with a little pepper, a generous pinch of salt, and 1 ½ teaspoons olive oil and brush this mixture onto the portobello slices. Place a heavy-bottomed frying pan over low heat. Put the portobello slices alongside each other in the pan, and allow them to dry slightly (about 5 minutes). Turn regularly.

Meanwhile, put the Raw Burgers on a piece of baking paper or aluminium foil that you've placed on the worktop and flatten them slightly. Top each Burger with a portobello slice and 1 sage leaf. Fasten the sage leaves to the portobello slices with the cocktail sticks, then press these slices firmly into the Burger.

Divide 75 grams margarine over 2 large frying pans. Melt over fairly high heat and wait until it starts to brown. Put the Burger saltimboccas alongside each other in the pans with the portobello-sage side down, and fry them for 3 to 4 minutes until nicely browned. Turn the saltimboccas, add the portobello chunks to the pans, squeeze the garlic into the pan through a garlic press, and fry for another 2 minutes. Turn the portobello chunks occasionally. Now put everything into one pan. Turn up the heat to the highest setting. Then pour in the wine and allow it to bubble briefly. Stir in the remaining margarine. Turn the heat down again and allow to cook gently for 2 to 3 minutes. Taste the wine gravy, and season with salt and pepper.

Meanwhile, in another pan, add enough olive oil to cover the bottom of the pan, then heat. Have a piece of kitchen paper ready. Put 4 to 5 sage leaves into the hot olive oil and fry them until crisp (takes less than 1 minute). Drain on kitchen paper while you fry the rest of the sage.

Place the Burger saltimboccas on warm plates or a platter along with the portobello chunks and the wine gravy, and sprinkle with the crispy sage leaves.

Translated literally, saltimbocca means 'leap into the mouth' – which shows just how delectable this Italian dish is! What could be a more fitting podium for our iconic vegan Raw Burger than this tasty tribute to Roman cuisine? *Buonissimo*!

4 servings (main dish) at least 45 minutes

SOUVLAKI WITH VEGAN CHICKEN CHUNKS AND SWEET PEPPER

2 garlic cloves
2 packs (160 g each) vegan Chicken Chunks by The Vegetarian Butcher
1 ½ tbsp gyros spice mix (ready-made or homemade*)
olive oil
2 Romano peppers (sweet pointed peppers)
2 red onions

Also needed: 4 long skewers (if wood, soaked in water for 30 minutes); grill, griddle, or grill pan with a tall lid or barbecue with a lid

* Homemade gyros spice mix: Mix 1 tsp salt, ½ tsp dried oregano, 1 tsbp thyme, 1 tsp dried basil, 1 ½ tsp smoked paprika (powder), ¼ tsp freshly ground black pepper, 1-2 tsp cayenne pepper, 1 tsp ground cinnamon, 2 tsp ground cumin, 1 tsp onion powder, and 2 tsp garlic powder. This spice mix will stay good for months if you keep it in a clean container or jar with a lid.

Preheat the grill to the highest setting or light the barbecue far enough in advance so the coals will be red-hot.

Cut the peppers in half and remove the seeds. Cut into chunks. Peel the onions and cut into chunks.

Thread the marinated Chicken Chunks onto the skewers, alternating them with chunks of pepper and onion. Grill the souvlaki, covered with the lid, for 5 to 7 minutes until browned on all sides.

Tip: Good served with fries or flatbread and a Greek salad with vegan feta, olives, onion rings, pepper, and tzatziki: Peel and finely dice 2 cucumbers or grate them into a colander. Sprinkle with 2 tsp salt, mix, and allow to stand for 10 minutes. Squeeze out as much liquid as possible, and mix with 200 ml vegan yoghurt, 1 pressed garlic clove, ½ tsp smoked paprika (powder), 4 finely chopped mint leaves, and a splash of olive oil. Taste, and season with pepper and salt.

Souvlaki – Greek skewers – can be grilled indoors or outside on the barbecue. These skewers are often eaten folded into Greek pitta bread with some tzatziki – so, minus the (wooden) skewer). Although souvlaki is usually made without vegetables, we alternate the meat on the skewers with chunks of pepper and onion. Variety is the spice of life!

6 servings (main dish) 25 minutes

BLACKENED VEGAN CAJUN BURGERS WITH GREEN TOMATOES AND HERB BUTTER

1 juicy organic lime
3 green tomatoes
1 green (bell) pepper
1 red onion
3 sprigs of basil
100 g vegan margarine (room temperature)
3½–4 tbsp Cajun seasoning
freshly ground black pepper and salt
1 tbsp maple syrup
sunflower oil
6 vegan Raw Burgers by The Vegetarian Butcher
6 slices seeded wholegrain bread (sliced by hand)

Also needed: pastry brush; barbecue with red-hot coals or a hot grill, grill pan, or griddle

Grate the lime into a large bowl. Cut the lime in half and squeeze both halves into the bowl. For the herb butter, put 1 teaspoon of the lime zest-juice mixture into a small bowl. The rest of the lime mixture is for the salad.

Cut the tomatoes and pepper into pieces. Peel the onion, cut in half, and slice into half-moons. Remove the basil leaves from the stems. Chop the stems and tear the leaves into pieces.

For the herb butter, finely chop 2 pieces of pepper, 2 onion half-moons, and a few pieces of basil (stems and leaves). Mix with the grated lime zest and juice in the small bowl. Add the margarine and 1 to 2 teaspoons Cajun seasoning. Taste, and season with pepper, salt, and more Cajun seasoning if desired.

Mix the onion slices, tomato, pepper, the basil, the maple syrup, a little pepper, a pinch of salt, and 2 tablespoons sunflower oil into the remaining grated lime zest and juice in the large bowl. Taste the salad, and season with pepper and salt.

Sprinkle both sides of the Raw Burgers with the remaining Cajun seasoning. Use more if you like things hot, use less if you don't. Then brush both sides with a little oil.

Brush both sides of the bread slices with a little oil as well. Grill the Burgers on the hot barbecue or under the grill, on the griddle, or in a grill pan, turning, until they are extra dark. Then grill the bread slices. Place the grilled bread slices on plates or wooden boards, and top with the Cajun Burgers. Divide the herb butter over the Burgers, and serve with the tomato salad on the side.

The heart of Cajun cooking is in the American state of Louisiana, where they use a cooking technique that involves searing seasoned ingredients in a red-hot cast-iron pan until they're nearly black. Bursting with flavour!

6 servings (main dish) 1 hour

MINI VEGAN BURGER ROULADES WITH MUSTARD AND DILL

½ leek
1 bunch (about 15 g) dill
75 g vegan margarine
90 g panko (Japanese breadcrumbs)
1 tsp smoked paprika (powder)
1 tbsp mustard
freshly ground black pepper and salt
6 vegan Raw Burgers by The Vegetarian Butcher

Also needed: 6 sheets (about 15 x 15 cm) baking paper; butcher's twine; a small roasting tin greased with vegan margarine

Preheat the oven to 180 °C. Slice the leek in half lengthwise, wash under the cold tap, and pat nice and dry with kitchen paper. Finely chop the leek and the dill.

Melt 30 grams margarine in a frying pan and stir-fry the finely chopped leek over fairly low heat for 3 minutes. Increase the heat to high, add 40 grams (a little less than half) panko and stir-fry for 2 minutes. Turn off the heat. Stir in the dill, the paprika, and the mustard. Taste, and season with pepper and salt.

Place the 6 sheets of baking paper side by side on the worktop. Sprinkle the remaining panko over the sheets, distributing evenly. Place a Raw Burger on each of the sheets, and flatten them slightly.

Divide the leek-herb mixture over the Burgers. Roll them up slowly with the help of a scraper or metal spatula. Place them on the baking paper seam-side down. Wrap a piece of butcher's twine around the roulades in 3 or 4 places and tie to fasten. Put the mini roulades in a roasting tin.

Distribute the remaining margarine over the mini roulades. Pour a generous splash of water (about 75 millilitres) into the roasting tin. Bake the mini roulades in the hot oven for about 25 minutes until browned and cooked through. Place on warm plates.

Tip: Good served with fluffy mashed potatoes mixed with fresh spinach or rucola. You can replace the leeks with spring onions or shallots, and the dill with chervil or parsley. And you can also add chopped olives, capers, and/or dried tomatoes.

With our meaty vegan Raw Burger, you can make mouth-watering roulades in no time for your next dinner party. Go ahead – you can steak your reputation on them!

BRAGARD

‘Food traditions are so important because they help preserve your culture.’

Asimakis Chaniotis is Greek, and executive chef at restaurant Pied à Terre in London. The Michelin-starred restaurant is frequently praised for its vegan menu.

I received The Vegetarian Butcher's products a few weeks back. They're terrific, and I'm already using them in our restaurant. My guests have responded very positively. The Burgers were the first thing I took home. I made them and thought, wow, this is delicious, not too heavy – I could eat this every night. A sort of evolution in plant-based meat.

At Pied à Terre we offer a ten-course vegan option alongside our regular tasting menu, but there was no actual moment when I decided to go in a different direction. We simply noticed that there was a demand for plant-based food. I'm from Greece, and in my country, we eat red meat once a week. On the other days we eat lentil soup, pasta, stuffed vegetables, or beans baked in the oven. So for me, plant-based cooking comes naturally. Nowadays, half of the menus we sell are vegan.

For me, food traditions are so important because they help preserve your culture. There's nothing wrong with globalization, but if someone goes to Spain and eats a hamburger, they are not really choosing for Spain. Every country should honour its food traditions and at the same time dare to create new variations that will carry these traditions forward into the modern age. I believe that our behaviour is driven by memories and traditions – I'm an omnivore because my mother used to give me lamb chops. If she had given me broccoli, then my childhood memory would probably have been of *that*. And thus, many people alive in a hundred years' time will never have experienced meat as children, and so will have no desire to revisit those lamb chops on special occasions. Their memories will be different than mine, and so will their traditions.

I think that The Vegetarian Butcher's ambition to become the world's largest butcher is a wonderful aim, and flavour will most certainly play a crucial role.

Although I've never felt the need to replicate meat, there is definitely a demand for it. Our regular menu has a course with heritage carrots prepared in various ways, topped with a piece of fried turbot. In the plant-based menu, I replace the fish with a mixture of vegan Raw Burger (soft texture, lightly seasoned) and chopped vegetarian Meatballs (firm texture, highly seasoned). This is also the recipe I'm contributing to this book.

ASIMAKIS COOKS: **HERITAGE CARROTS WITH VEGAN MEAT SLICES**

HERITAGE CARROTS WITH VEGAN MEAT SLICES

2 packs (170 g each) vegetarian Meatballs by The Vegetarian Butcher
3 vegan Raw Burgers by The Vegetarian Butcher
250 g orange carrots, plus 12 small ones for the garnish
250 g purple carrots, plus 12 small ones for the garnish
2 pieces of star anise
2 sprigs of tarragon
salt
sugar
12 small yellow carrots, plus a few sprigs of carrot top greens
1 tbsp sesame seeds
1 tbsp poppy seeds
1 nori sheet (Asian supermarket)
1 tbsp (about 3 g) kombu granules (Asian supermarket)
olive oil
½ tsp tandoori masala mix*

Also needed: food processor along with the plastic and metal blade attachment; if you have one, a sous vide cooker and 5 bags; kitchen thermometer; a new scouring pad; grinder or mortar

Put the Meatballs and Raw Burger into a food processor equipped with the plastic blade, and grind them into a smooth thick paste. Line a small baking tray with baking paper. Shape the mixture into a 3-cm thick rectangle, and smooth the top and sides. Place the tray in the freezer for 30 minutes. If you don't plan to use it immediately, transfer the tray to the fridge until you put it in the oven.

Clean the 250 grams orange and 250 grams purple carrots, and cut them into thin slices. Place the sliced orange carrots into a sous vide bag or small saucepan, and the purple carrots into another bag or pan. To each bag or pan, add 1 star anise, a sprig of tarragon, a pinch of salt, and a pinch of sugar. Vacuum-seal the bags, or add enough water to the saucepans to cover the carrots. To prepare using a sous vide cooker: Heat 2 litres of water to 85 °C. Place the bags in the water, and cook the carrots until tender (10 to 15 minutes). To prepare in a saucepan: Bring the water to a boil, and cook over low heat until the carrots are tender (10 to 15 minutes).

Now prepare the small orange, purple, and yellow carrots for the garnish. Using the scouring pad, carefully rub the skin off of all these carrots, then rinse them under running water. Place them into 3 plastic bags or saucepans according to colour. Add a pinch of salt or sugar to each bag or pan. Vacuum-seal the bags, or add enough water to the saucepans to cover the carrots. To prepare using a sous vide cooker: Heat 2 litres of water to 85 °C. Place the bags in the water, and cook the carrots until tender, about 6 to 8 minutes. To prepare in a saucepan: Bring to a boil and cook for 6 to 8 minutes.

Meanwhile, toast the sesame seeds and poppy seeds together in a small dry frying pan over low heat. Using the grinder or mortar, grind the nori and the kombu granules into a fine powder.

Now prepare the orange and the purple carrot cream. In 2 separate batches, use the food processor equipped with the metal blade to puree the tender orange carrot slices (250 grams) and the purple carrot slices (250 grams) into an orange and a purple cream. Add salt to taste.

Cut each of the small carrots into 3 pieces; one end of each piece should be flat (to allow it to stand) and one end should be cut on the diagonal (see picture).

Half an hour before serving, preheat the oven to 170 °C. Lightly brush the mince rectangle with olive oil. Place the tray into the preheated oven, and bake for 8 to 10 minutes.

Meanwhile, reheat the 2 carrot creams (sous vide or in saucepans). Carefully cut the mince rectangle into 8 neat slices, about 3 x 7 cm. (Trimmings are very tasty in a sandwich.)

Presentation: In the centre of 4 warm flat plates, place 4 small scoops of carrot cream (2 orange and 2 purple) side by side, alternating between colours. Using a spoon, spread the scoops of cream into thin lines towards one side of the plate. Then arrange 2 rows of orange, yellow, and purple carrot pieces on each plate. Place the mince slices alongside the pieces of carrot. Sprinkle them first with the nori and kombu mixture, then with the sesame and poppyseeds. Garnish with small sprigs of carrot top greens. Dust one corner of the plate with the tandoori masala mixture.

***Tandoori masala mixture: Dry-roast 20 g cumin seeds, 7 g coriander seeds, 4 g cloves, and 1 cinnamon stick in a pan over low heat until the spices begin to release their aroma. Remove the mixture from the heat and allow it to cool. In a coffee grinder or mortar, grind the cooled spices along with 4 g ground ginger, 4 g garlic powder, 4 g red chilli powder, 4 g turmeric powder, 4 g mace powder, 4 g salt, and ¼ tsp orange food colouring (optional). Store the mixture in an airtight container for up to 6 to 8 weeks.**

6 servings (main dish) 1 hour and 20 minutes

VEGAN BURGER OSSO BUCO WITH GREMOLATA

1 large onion
2 garlic cloves
1 medium carrot
4 celery stalks
1 bunch (about 15 g) fresh Italian herbs (with bay leaf)
3 tbsp flour
freshly ground black pepper and salt
olive oil
6 vegan Raw Burgers by The Vegetarian Butcher
200 ml dry white wine
500 ml vegetable stock
20 g dried mixed mushrooms
1 large organic lemon
1 bunch (about 15 g) flat-leaf parsley

Also needed: large casserole (Dutch oven) with lid

Peel and finely chop the onion and garlic. Peel and thinly slice the carrot. Cut the celery stalks into thin arches. Remove the leaves from the sprigs of herbs and finely chop. Leave the bay leaf whole.

Sprinkle the flour onto a large plate and mix with about 1 teaspoon coarsely ground pepper. Add a generous splash of olive oil to the casserole and place over medium heat. Dip the Raw Burgers lightly in the seasoned flour to coat, and fry them for about 2 to 3 minutes, turning, until lightly browned on both sides. Remove them from the pan and place them on the inverted lid. Add another splash of olive oil to the pan. Then add the vegetables and half of the garlic. Sprinkle with a little salt and stir-fry for 4 minutes until they start to brown. Stir in the herbs and the rest of the seasoned flour.

Increase the heat to high. Stir as you pour in the wine. Once the wine has stopped bubbling, pour in the stock. Bring to a boil while stirring. Add the dried mushrooms (don't soak them in advance!). Return the Burgers to the pan, cover, and allow to simmer for 1 hour.

Meanwhile, make the gremolata: Grate the zest of the lemon into a small bowl. Finely chop the parsley and stir it into the lemon zest along with the remaining garlic.

Taste the Burger osso buco sauce and season with pepper and salt. Top with the gremolata just before serving.

Osso buco, a Milanese meat dish, has long been made without tomatoes. We're happy to uphold this tradition – all the more because it allows our vegan Raw Burger to shine, surrounded by a richly flavoured vegetable sauce and served with the customary gremolata. Tradition never dies.

SACRIF

CE NOTHING

4 servings (main dish) 20 minutes

BARBECUED VEGAN BURGER WITH CHIMICHURRI

1 small red onion
3 garlic cloves
1 small red chilli pepper
1 tsp mustard seed
1 bunch (about 15 g) flat-leaf parsley
1 tsp dried oregano
2 tsp ground cumin
apple cider vinegar
10 tbsp sunflower oil, plus extra
freshly ground black pepper and salt
4 vegan Raw Burgers by The Vegetarian Butcher

Also needed: mortar and pestle, liquidizer (blender) or hand blender with blending cup; barbecue with red-hot coals

Peel the onion and garlic, cut the red chilli pepper in half, remove the stem, seeds, and membranes, and finely chop. Grind or process the onion, garlic, red chilli pepper (the more you use, the hotter the sauce), mustard seed, parsley, and oregano until coarsely ground.

Add 1 teaspoon cumin and a generous splash of vinegar (it should be nice and wet). Stir in the sunflower oil a tablespoon at a time. Add pepper and salt to taste. The chimichurri tastes even better if it stands for a few hours or overnight.

Light your barbecue on time!

Mix 1 ½ teaspoons pepper with the rest of the cumin, 1 tablespoon chimichurri, and a small splash of sunflower oil. Rub this into the Raw Burgers.

Grill the Burgers on the grilling rack for about 8 to 10 minutes, turning, until they're browned and cooked through. Transfer to 4 wooden boards and serve with the rest of chimichurri.

Tip: Delicious served with grilled corn on the cob, bread, and a chunky salad with (bell) pepper.

This recipe for vegan Raw Burgers with chimichurri will take your grilling to a whole new level. Chimichurri is both tangy and spicy and actually more of a dressing than a sauce. In a number of South American countries, it's traditionally served with grilled meat. A real flavour bomb for all of our highly esteemed barbecue fans.

4 servings (main dish) 25 minutes

VEGAN BURGER TOURNEDOS WITH MUSHROOMS AND RED WINE SAUCE

4 vegan Raw Burgers by The Vegetarian Butcher
freshly ground black pepper and salt
1 shallot
1 garlic clove
200 g white mushrooms
5 sprigs of thyme
50 g vegan margarine
200 ml red wine
200 ml vegetable stock
200 ml vegan cooking cream

Put the Raw Burgers on a cutting board, circle each Burger with your hands, and squeeze in and up to form tournedos towers of 6 to 7 cm Ø and 3 to 4 cm high. Sprinkle the Burger tournedos with pepper.

Peel and finely chop the shallot and garlic. Clean the mushrooms. Cut large ones into four and cut small ones in half. Remove the thyme leaves from the stems and chop them until fairly coarse.

Heat the margarine in a frying pan over high heat and when it starts to brown, fry the Burger tournedos for about 6 minutes until nicely browned all over. Remove from the pan and cover with a lid to keep them warm. Sprinkle the shallot, garlic, thyme, and mushrooms into the fat in the frying pan and stir-fry for 3 minutes.

Pour the wine into the mushroom mixture. Allow to bubble for a moment, then add the stock. Stir in the cooking cream, and allow the sauce to simmer gently over fairly low heat for a few minutes. Taste, and season with pepper and salt. Return the Burger tournedos to the pan and heat them in the sauce for 5 minutes. If the sauce gets too thick, keep adding small amounts of water as needed, shaking the pan to blend in the liquid.

Tip: These are traditionally served with pan-fried new potatoes and broccoli. Would you like to win the supper sweepsteaks? Use a peeler to slice 4 long, thin ribbons of carrot, cook them briefly, wrap them around the tournedos, and fasten with butcher's twine.

These tournedos are an elegant classic. Traditionally, they are wrapped in bacon before cooking. Instead, we decided to raise the steaks, so we came up with this vegan Raw Burger tournedos hack.

4 servings (main dish) 1 hour

SUNDAY ROAST VEGAN CHICKEN BREAST AND SPICY APPLESAUCE

1 kg floury potatoes
olive oil
freshly ground black pepper and salt
2 cooking apples (such as Bramleys) or other sweet-tart apples
1 organic lime
4 tbsp granulated sugar
small piece of red chilli pepper
½ tsp curry powder
3 (bell) peppers (1 red, 1 yellow, and 1 green)
1 yellow (summer squash) or green courgette (zucchini)
12 green asparagus spears
4 vegan Chicken Breasts by The Vegetarian Butcher
small bunch of mixed fresh herbs (such as thyme, rosemary, and sage)

Also needed: roasting tin; grater

Preheat the oven to 200 °C.

Peel the potatoes; cut small ones in half and large ones into quarters. Put the potatoes in the roasting tin. Pour in a generous splash of olive oil, sprinkle the potatoes with a little pepper and salt, and mix together well. Place the roasting tin in the middle of the oven and first roast the potatoes for 25 minutes. Turn them twice as they cook.

Meanwhile, peel, quarter, and core the apples and cut the quarters into chunks. Put the chunks into a small pan. Grate the zest of the lime onto the apples in the pan, then cut the lime in half and squeeze in the juice of both halves. Stir in the sugar, red chilli pepper, and the curry powder. Add 80–100 millilitres of water, bring to a boil, and cook over fairly high heat until the apples break down into a puree. Stir frequently, and add a little more water if the apples are not yet tender but the liquid has evaporated. Set aside, and remove the piece of chilli pepper at the end.

While the apples are cooking, prepare the vegetables. Cut the peppers and courgettes into chunks. If necessary, cut off the woody ends of the asparagus spears.

After the potatoes have baked for 25 minutes, stir the vegetables into the potatoes in the roasting tin. Tuck the sprigs of herbs and the Chicken Breasts into this mixture, and sprinkle the Chicken Breasts with a little pepper. Put the roasting tin back in the oven and bake for another 20 minutes.

Serve the roast Chicken Breast, potatoes, and vegetables with the spicy applesauce.

The sky's the limit when it comes to the vegetables you can use for this roast. Root vegetables take longer to cook. So make sure you put them in the oven at the same time as the potatoes. No need to chicken out on Sunday roast!

CLASSICS

‘I’m the son of a butcher, and when I was growing up, meat took centre stage. But I have no doubt that plant-based foods will see strong growth over the coming years.’

Erik van Loo is the chef and owner of restaurant Parkheuvel in the Dutch city of Rotterdam. Even this classically trained chef with two Michelin stars to his name has no doubt that the future will be more plant-based.

Because we have an experienced team here at Parkheuvel, with a bit of advanced notice we can create a beautiful vegetarian menu without much effort. However, when you remove eggs, meat, and dairy from the equation, this requires a very different approach to the dishes. Of course, it's also possible to make something that resembles meat, like our steak tartare made from watermelon and our dry-aged beetroot, which we first cook and then allow to dry. I've tried The Vegetarian Butcher's products, and I thought the taste was amazing. You have to make sure the texture is right, and use spices that people associate with classic meat dishes. For this cookbook I'm making one of my own classics – ravioli, but with a filling from The Vegetarian Butcher. The pasta is exactly the same, and I think the filling will taste the same too.

I don't think special occasions and celebrations have to involve eating large quantities of animal meat. This tradition is gradually disappearing. What I see and hear around me shows that in people's homes there is less of a focus on meat. At Parkheuvel, we used to have a vegetarian menu alongside our regular menu, and we suddenly noticed that no one was ordering it. Now we have gone back to a classical menu that we can adapt for those who prefer a vegetarian version. Although my son always jokes that those people can't eat in our restaurant because our chairs are upholstered in leather. Vegetarians account for fewer than five percent of our guests, which may have to do with the fact that Rotterdam is still a city of harbour workers. People here are slower to embrace new things than those in the other major Dutch cities. I'm the son of a butcher, and when I was growing up, meat took centre stage. But I have no doubt that plant-based foods will see strong growth over the coming years. This development will result from changing demand. Just look at Eleven Madison Park*** in New York, which has now gone completely vegan: you only do something like that if there is enough demand. Veganism has been portrayed lately as uber-hip, and that's now bearing fruit.

ERIK COOKS: **SIGNATURE RAVIOLI WITH VEGAN CHICKEN CHUNKS**

SIGNATURE RAVIOLI WITH VEGAN CHICKEN CHUNKS

FOR THE MUSHROOM CRÈME SAUCE
1 shallot
250 g white mushrooms
splash of olive oil
25 ml white wine
300 ml vegetable stock
300 ml vegan (cooking) cream
freshly ground black pepper and salt

FOR THE RAVIOLI
1 pack (160 g) vegan Chicken Chunks by The Vegetarian Butcher
100 g mixed vegetables such as carrot, celeriac (celery root), courgette (zucchini)
300 g mixed mushrooms
1 shallot
olive oil
white wine
100 ml vegetable stock
100 ml vegan (cooking) cream
1 tsp truffle tapenade
a few drops of truffle oil
freshly ground black pepper and salt
24 wonton wrappers (thawed; freezer section, Asian supermarket)

PLUS
oil for deep-frying
2 salsifies (scorzonera)
12 mixed mushrooms
15 chives

Also needed: hand blender; pan for deep-frying or deep fryer; kitchen thermometer; round cutter (about 10 cm Ø)

4 servings (appetizer or side dish) 1 hour and 10 minutes

Start with the mushroom crème sauce: peel and finely chop the shallot. Clean the mushrooms. Heat a splash of olive oil in a saucepan over medium heat. Add the shallot and mushrooms, and fry for about 3 minutes until translucent. Increase the heat to high, and deglaze with the white wine. Pour in the vegetable stock. Bring to a boil and allow the liquid to reduce by half. Stir the cream into the mushroom mixture, and bring to a boil again. With the hand blender, blend the sauce in the pan until smooth. Pass the sauce through a sieve, and season with pepper and salt. Set aside.

Make the ravioli: cut the vegan Chicken Chunks into small pieces, and dice the mixed vegetables and mushrooms. Peel and finely chop the shallot. Heat a splash of olive oil in a large frying pan over fairly low heat and fry the diced vegetables and shallot for about 4 minutes. Stir in the Chicken Chunks. Increase the heat to high, and deglaze with a splash of white wine. Add the stock. Allow the liquid to reduce somewhat. Pour in the cream. Bring to a boil and reduce the liquid until the mixture has thickened nicely. Add the truffle tapenade, a few drops of truffle oil, and pepper and salt. Allow to cool.

Place 12 wonton wrappers on a cutting board. Put a generous spoonful of the Chicken Chunk filling in the middle of each wrapper, staying back 3 cm from the edges. Brush the edges with a little bit of cold water. Immediately cover with a second wonton wrapper, and press the edges together. Make sure there is no air inside the ravioli. Cut the ravioli into rounds with the cutter, or cut them with a clean scissors, or leave them square if you like. Cover the ravioli well (leaving a little space between each one) and put them in the fridge until you're ready to cook them.

Heat enough oil for deep-frying to 170 °C. (Use a kitchen thermometer if you're deep-frying in an ordinary pan.) Peel the salsify and slice into long, very thin slices. Pat them dry with kitchen paper. Deep-fry the slices in 6 batches until they are light brown and crisp. Allow to drain on kitchen paper.

Cut the mushrooms into large chunks. Snip the chives into large pieces.

Fill a deep pan with water until it is three-quarters full, then add a little salt and a splash of olive oil, and bring to a boil. Meanwhile, heat a splash of olive oil in a frying pan over high heat and fry the mushroom chunks for 2 to 3 minutes until light brown.

Cook the ravioli (no more than 4 at a time) for a few minutes until done (that is when they float to the surface). Remove them from the pan with a skimmer and keep them warm under a lid while you're cooking the rest.

Spoon half of the fried mushrooms into the middle of 4 warmed deep plates. Arrange the cooked ravioli on top of the mushrooms. Spoon the mushroom crème sauce around the ravioli, then add the remaining fried mushrooms to the plate. Garnish with the pieces of chive and deep-fried salsify.

4 servings (main dish) 40 minutes

STUFFED VEGAN CHICKEN BREASTS WITH CHESTNUTS AND ORANGE

1 onion
2 garlic cloves
50 g vegan margarine
400 g pre-cooked chestnuts (jar, tin, or vacuum-packed)
1 orange
1 bunch (about 15 g) mixed herbs (parsley, thyme, and chives)
200 g vegan cream cheese
freshly ground black pepper and salt
4 vegan Chicken Breasts by The Vegetarian Butcher

Also needed: grater; butcher's twine; roasting tin; palette knife or metal spatula

Peel and finely chop the onion and garlic. Heat half of the margarine in a large frying pan over low heat and stir-fry the onion and garlic for 4 minutes until translucent.

Cut the chestnuts into pieces and put them in a bowl. Wash the orange and finely grate the zest into the bowl with the chestnuts. Add the onion and garlic. Remove the leaves from the sprigs of parsley and thyme and finely chop them along with the chives. Add three-quarters of the herbs to the bowl with the chestnuts. Stir in the cream cheese. Season with pepper and salt.

Cut each Chicken Breast into 5 thick slices. Put the slices back together in neat rows on pieces of baking paper. Place 2 long pieces of butcher's twine (3 times the length of the Chicken Breasts) lengthwise underneath each one. Place a generous spoonful of the chestnut mixture in between every Chicken Breast slice. Press the slices together firmly, tightly wrap them with the butcher's twine, and tie them closed. Using a palette knife or metal spatula, carefully transfer the stuffed Chicken Breasts to the roasting tin, and top them with the remaining margarine, divided into small chunks. Put them in the fridge until use.

Juice the orange.

Thirty-five minutes before you would like to serve, preheat the oven to 200 °C. Put the roasting tin in the oven and bake the Chicken Breasts for about 25 minutes until light brown. After 15 minutes, sprinkle on the orange juice.

Tip: Tasty served with red or green cabbage, parsnip puree, and cranberry compote. For a little variety, try adding coarsely chopped dried cranberries to the chestnut mixture.

This stuffed vegan Chicken Breast with chestnuts and orange is an excellent choice for a dinner party or an extensive lunch for family and friends. Elegant, festive, and utterly delicious! You don't even have to work around the cluck – this dish is ready to serve in just forty minutes.

INDEX

NIJGH
CUISINE

Nijgh Cuisine is a division of Nijgh & Van Ditmar

Concept: Amadea Boneschansker, Valerie Vos, José van Mil, Fleur van Mil, and Nijgh Cuisine
Texts: The Vegetarian Butcher
Recipes and food styling: Pepper & Salt | José van Mil and Fleur van Mil
Photography: Remko Kraaijeveld
Translation: Colleen Higgins
Editor: Françoise Takken-Kaminker
Portrait of Jonnie & Thérèse Boer: De Librije
Portrait of Asimakis Chaniotis: Pied à Terre
Portrait of James Goodyear: Adam's Restaurant
Portrait of Josita Hartanto: Lucky Leek
Portrait of Andrew Pern: Bailey Cooper Photography
Portrait of Ricky Saward: Seven Swans
Styling: De Stijlbrouwerij | Jan Willem van Riel
Illustrations: Deborah van der Schaaf
Design: Annelies Dollekamp

NUR 440 / ISBN 978 90 388 1187 1

www.thevegetarianbutcher.co.uk
www.nijghenvanditmar.nl